ONE WEEK LOAN

0 8 MAY 2003

GRAHAM GREENE

Graham Greene

Peter Mudford

Northcote House

in association with
The British Council

First published in 1996 by Northcote House Publishers Ltd, Plymbridge House, Estover Road, Plymouth PL6 7PZ, United Kingdom.
Tel: +44 (0) 1752 202300. Fax: +44 (0) 1752 202330.

British Library Cataloguing-in-Publication Data
A catalogue record for this book is available from the British Library

ISBN 0 7463 0758 6

Typeset by PDQ Typesetting, Newcastle-Under-Lyme
Printed and bound in the United Kingdom

for
LUKE

Contents

Acknowledgements   viii

Biographical Outline   ix

Abbreviations and References   x

Prologue   1

1   Portraits and Self-Portraits   2

2   Travels, Dreams, and Films   11

3   'A writer who happens to be a Catholic'   21

4   Politics and Betrayal   37

5   Abandonment and Survival   50

Notes   59

Select Bibliography   62

Index   68

Acknowledgements

I am grateful to the Estate of Graham Greene and Penguin Books for permission to quote from his works; to Bodley Head (Random House) to quote from M.-F. Allain, *The Other Man: Conversations with Graham Greene*, translated by Guido Waldman; to Jonathan Cape (Random House) for permission to quote from Norman Sherry, *The Life of Graham Greene*, vols i and ii; and to HarperCollins (Fount) to quote from Leopoldo Duran: *Graham Greene: Friend and Brother*, translated by Euan Cameron. I am also grateful to Dr. David Atkinson for his help in compiling the index.

Biographical Outline

1904   Born at Berkhamsted, Hertfordshire, son of Charles Henry Greene, History and Classics master, later Headmaster at Berkhamsted School.

1912–22 Berkhamsted School.

1922–5 Balliol College, Oxford.

1926   Sub-editor on *The Times*. Becomes a Roman Catholic.

1927   Marries Vivien Dayrell-Browning.

1929   His first novel, *The Man Within*, is published. Resigns from *The Times* to become a novelist.

1932   *Stamboul Train*.

1934   Travels to Liberia with his cousin Barbara.

1935   Film critic for the *Spectator* (till 1940).

1936   *Journey without Maps*.

1937   Co-editor and film critic of *Night and Day*. Travels to Mexico.

1938   *Brighton Rock*. Meets Dorothy Glover.

1939   *The Lawless Roads*.

1940   *The Power and the Glory*.

1941–3 Intelligence Services in Sierra Leone.

1944–8 Director of Eyre and Spottiswoode, Publishers, London.

1946   Meets Catherine Walston.

1948   *The Heart of the Matter*.

1951   *The End of the Affair*.

1952–   Begins to travel widely: Indo-China, Kenya, Haiti, Cuba, Congo, Paraguay, Panama, Spain. Continues to publish novels, stories, and plays. The titles and dates are to be found in the bibliography.

1961   Meets Yvonne Cloetta, who will become his companion until the end of his life.

1966   Goes to live in France, first in Paris, later in Antibes.

1991   Dies in Vevey, Switzerland.

Abbreviations and References

All quotations from Greene's Works are taken from the Penguin Twentieth Century Classics editions.

BOC	*A Burnt-Out Case*
BR	*Brighton Rock*
Com.	*The Comedians*
CS	*Collected Short Stories*
HC	*The Honorary Consul*
HF	*The Human Factor*
HM	*The Heart of the Matter*
JM	*Journey without Maps*
LR	*The Lawless Roads*
MQ	*Monsignor Quixote*
OMH	*Our Man in Havana*
PD	*The Pleasure Dome*
PG	*The Power and the Glory*
QA	*The Quiet American*
SL	*A Sort of Life*
SR	*A Sense of Reality*
TA	*Travels with my Aunt*
WE	*Ways of Escape*
WO	*A World of my Own*

Prologue

Graham Greene was born in 1904 and died in 1991. His life covered eighty-seven years of the twentieth century. As his fame grew, it brought him access to statesmen, churchmen, and the press in the many countries. Travel was essential to him, in particular to places where danger existed. His gifts as a story-teller were inspired by the political and moral conflicts of the twentieth century. In style he regarded simplicity as the central virtue. This combination of representativeness and accessibility gave him an immense popular appeal, enabling him to invade the public imagination as few writers in our time have done. This book is intended not as a survey of all his work, but as an attempt to account for his representativeness within the culture of the twentieth century.

1

Portraits and Self-Portraits

The first volume of Graham Greene's authorized biography by Norman Sherry was published in 1989. Before the second was completed in 1993, Greene had died. In 1994, an unauthorized biography by Michael Shelden, written without access to unpublished material and letters, appeared, as did a portrait by Fr Leopoldo Duran, a Catholic priest who had been a friend and travelling companion of Greene's over more than twenty years. Fr Duran was alone with Greene when he died, after receiving the final rites of the Church in which he claimed to be an agnostic. His portrait has the advantage of conversations in moments of pleasure and relaxation. But Greene lived his life in many rooms; an intensely private man, who disliked interviews, he warned his biographers that those who wanted to depict his life would face an almost impossible task, as he had so energetically covered or even distorted his tracks. 'If anybody ever tries to write a biography of me, how complicated they are going to find it, and how misled they are going to be.'[1]

The novelist whose narratives often derived tension from the theme of the pursuer and the pursued, the hunter and the hunted; the man whose close connection with the Intelligence Services may perhaps never be entirely revealed, lived in shadows of his own psychological making. As Yvonne Cloetta, the woman who remained his close companion during the last quarter of his life, wrote in her introduction to his posthumously published dream diary, *A World of my Own* (1992), 'Graham guarded his privacy as fiercely as he respected the privacy of others' (*WO*, p. vii). In this, the ordinary English reticence of Greene's generation and class was fused with the extraordinary harbouring of the sources of his creative talent. Secrecy preserved the interest of what he was making, as it also saved him from the boredom by which he claimed to be tormented throughout his life. Life and art were involved in an intricate web of concealment and disclosure, where in the end only God could be the true detective. This idea has shaped the conscience of the Catholic novels; but in *The Honorary Consul* (1973) he returned to it as a way of demarcating political and literary change.

> There were no detective stories in the age of faith – an interesting point when you think of it. God used to be the only detective when people believed in Him. He was law. He was order. He was good. Like your Sherlock Holmes ... But now people like the General make law and order. Electric shocks on the genitals ... I prefer the detective. I prefer God.' (*HC* 208)

The preference expressed by a failed Catholic priest reflects Greene's own position – and his recognition of how deeply the contemporary world had changed, even in the twenty years since he had completed *The End of the Affair* (1951), his last 'Catholic' novel.

In the service of privacy, Greene was given to repetition of what he did not object to discussing. In this way he diverted attention from what he wished to conceal. All the most important things in a writer's life, he often declared, happened during the first sixteen years. In writing his own autobiography, *A Sort of Life* (1971), he stopped his narrative at the age of 27 – ostensibly to protect the privacy of those with whom he had been involved in his adult life. Norman Sherry has now pursued Greene to the age of 51, visiting the places and remaking the journeys which inspired much of his fiction. 'At this moment a person hitherto unknown to me, Norman Sherry, is busy writing my biography. The poor man! Terrible things keep happening to him as he goes wherever I've been. He dogs my footsteps. He's been to the same lost Mexican villages. He's caught dysentery in the very Mexican town I caught it in 1938' (*SL* 17). Although Greene cooperated in this venture, he expressed the desire to die before it was finished; and as usual was clever enough to do so. (The interest of Sherry's biography comes largely from other sources.) Fr Duran's account of journeys in Spain (and occasional meetings until the day of Greene's death) provide the background to the writing of *Monsignor Quixote*; but from Greene's life in Antibes, and elsewhere, he is excluded.

The desire to live in compartments which was essential to

3

Greene shaped the structure and content of his fictions, where being a double agent, or going double, in sexual or political terms gave the narrative the excitement he cherished in life as in art. But the interest of Greene's life does not lie just in the relation between the psychological and the creative, portrayed by Shelden as involving every kind of duplicity. It can be read too as illustrative of problems and preoccupations which have formed the consciousness of the twentieth century; and, for this, Greene himself, Sherry, and Duran have their special uses.

Greene was educated at Berkhamsted School, where his own father was Headmaster. The divided loyalty between home and school, symbolized by the green baize door which separated them, was exacerbated by the mental suffering which he experienced in lack of privacy (always essential to him); and by the cruelty of a bully called Carter, who helped to form in him that awareness of evil which later shaped his works of fiction. Carter also induced Wheeler, Greene's closest friend, to betray him. In this period of adolescent unhappiness, dominated by schoolboy fantasies of plots and counterplots, his obsession with subversion began to be formed: he became and remained deeply hostile to the authoritarian, whether it took the form of individual power or of State oppression; and this tension fostered his creative talent. ' "It has always been in the interest of the State to poison the psychological wells... to restrict human sympathy." In contrast, it is the story-teller's task "to elicit sympathy and a measure of understanding for those who lie outside the boundaries of State approval." '[2] More concretely, Greene's anti-authoritarianism expressed itself in a dislike of uniforms; and a temperament which never ceased to be protestant.

The balance of loyalty, whether to his father or to his class mates, was never clear. Loyalty itself was subverted, and its opposite could become a virtue. No side was always right; and the monitor of this had to be experience, not dogma. These strong but often clouded sympathies characterize much in the twentieth-century outlook, where conviction, whether in religion or politics or sexuality, has often registered a dark undertow, and existed within shifting parameters. The burden of this, however, is hard to bear; and in the young Greene it expressed itself in moods of black depression, suicidal tendencies, a desire to run away, and at the age of 16 the need for psychoanalysis. The attempted cure now seems as symptomatic as the condition, though Greene's father showed remarkably advanced views in permitting it in 1920. The analyst with whom Greene went to stay was a Jungian, and the major part of his treatment consisted of recalling or attempting to recall his dream of the previous night (when necessary he invented it). Whatever the effect of this therapy on his mental state at the time, dreams, and the recalling of them, continued to remain indispensable to his creative life. His novels frequently contained dreams, and were inspired by dreams, even at times by dreams which were apparently disconnected (see Chapter 2). As a writer, Greene's involvement with, and debt to, the subconscious, formed at an early age by deep instabilities of temperament, indicate another way in which his creative talent was to become representative. As writing served partly as a psychotherapy, dreams too could be a form of escape. 'You should dream more, Mr Wormold. Reality in our century is not something to be faced' (*OMH* 10).

The first two parts of Sherry's biography include the years of Graham Greene's rise to fame with *The Power and the Glory* (1940), *The Heart of the Matter* (1948), and *The End of the Affair* (1951). But they also chronicle that part of Greene's private life which he assiduously protected; his marriage to Vivienne (she later changed this to Vivien) Dayrell-Browning in 1927, their gradual estrangement, his prolonged relationship with Dorothy Glover, and his impassioned affair with Catherine Walston. In this narrative of prolonged, but none the less passing relationships we may also see something paradigmatic of the twentieth century. (In Greene's case, it would not be possible to speak of 'serial monogamy' because of his frequent resort to prostitutes, which was unconcealed, and his taste for brothels.) The importance for him of sex, as apparent in his fiction as in his life, touches too on his popular appeal; but unlike D. H. Lawrence, whose fictional depiction of sex Greene thought to be false, Greene's highly charged drives were not until late in his life separated from feelings of guilt which derived from his faith.

Greene's courtship of Vivien was beset by problems. As a Catholic, she did not want to marry a man who was not. In addition she shared with many deeply religious natures a fear of sex, which even led for a time to Greene proposing a celibate marriage. When Greene was converted to her faith at the age of

22, she agreed to marry him, though neither desired to have children. As he admitted later his true loyalty lay to Vivien and only secondly to the Church. But what began as an intellectual conversion for personal reasons became, after his experience of the persecution of Catholics in Mexico in 1938, an emotional conversion too.

He remained married to Vivien throughout his life, as he also remained in faith a Catholic. Like Evelyn Waugh, who was to stay a close friend until his death in 1951 in spite of the differences in their political outlook, Greene's career as a writer, and his hold on the popular imagination, was determined by his 'commitment' (a key word of literary criticism in the 1950s when Greene achieved fame). Even if he was neither in dogma nor in personal life a good Catholic, his Catholicism gave him a point of view and saved him from the amorphous pluralism of his time. Without his Catholicism, he would not have developed the distinctive voice and style on which his artistry, like that of all artists, depends. J. N. Moore in his biography of Elgar put it like this:

> The artist, like the rest of us, is torn by various desires competing within himself. But, unlike the rest of us, he makes each of those desires into an element for use in his art. Then he seeks to synthesize his elements all together to form a style. The sign of a successful synthesis is a unified and unique style plain for all to recognise.[3]

Greene's failure to be orthodox, to accept without questioning, resulted in an anguished individualism, symptomatic of the twentieth century. A writer needs passionate intensity, an obsession with the craft of writing; and Greene had these in full measure. In style the anguish was always tempered by the narrative control. But the eccentric, rather than concentric nature of his convictions saved him too from an ideological rigidity which would have diminished the human sympathy of his writing. 'A writer must be able to cross over, to "change sides at the drop of a hat. He stands for the victims and the victims change." That obliges him to violate his faith or his political opinions, to be unscrupulous, but it's indispensable."[4] Dostoevsky's belief that man could not live without pity was shared by Greene, and extended to a metaphysical belief in the mercy of God, of which it was a reflection. Michael Shelden in his hostile biography sees the ambivalences in Greene's life as grounds for disliking the man;

6

more importantly, they are grounds for regarding him as a representative artist.

Greene had two children by Vivien; but early in the marriage he discovered the impossibility of fidelity. A tension between his faith and his way of life was set up which was essential to his creative life. What he described as the splinter of ice in his heart as a writer separated him from wife and children, and reflected the deeper need and obsession with his art. (His life, as he admitted, was his books.) His marriage to Vivien for all practical purposes was finished by 1939, when he began living much of the time with Dorothy Glover. His sense of responsibility to both Vivien and Dorothy was further intensified when in 1946 he met Catherine Walston, who was to transform his emotional and creative life. As with Vivien, though in the reverse direction, Catholicism was to act as a catalyst.

Catherine Walston was married to a wealthy landowner, and had five young children. Her sexual relationship with her husband had ended; she was determined 'not to be chaste and yet was deeply religious'. Greene's Catholic books had attracted her interest, and she wrote to ask him to act as her 'godfather' at the time of her conversion. Ironically, it was Vivien who was to make the arrangements. And, complaisant as Harry Walston was, their affair was to cause him great grief.

Without Catherine Walston, *The Heart of the Matter* would not have been completed, *The End of the Affair* would never have been written, and his subsequent writing would have been very different. She revived his religious sense, on which he believed all art depended. He was, he told her, 'a much better Catholic in mortal sin'.[5] This paradox expressed an anguish which he could not resolve, and which is present in many of the relationships of Greene's later fiction. 'I find the idea [of mortal sin] difficult to accept because it must by definition be committed in defiance of God. I doubt whether a man making love to a woman ever does so with the intention of defying God.'[6] As the affair continued intermittently and he was besieged by jealousies, fears, and anxieties, Greene tried to persuade Catherine to leave her husband and to marry him. But, although he claimed he 'felt no wrong in this love for her'[7], he could not overcome her sense of religious guilt. He increasingly came to see that she would be happier and her life at home more peaceful without him. She was worried by his sexual energy, and the demands he made on her, which, as before his marriage to Vivien, he offered to give up. In spite of all this she felt a responsibility to him; and he loved her with an intensity which inspired his writing. 'Almost all my Catholic writing has been done since I knew you.'[8] When finally their lives began to take separate ways, Greene was to find in Yvonne Cloetta, also married, a companion for his last twenty-five years. But they never lived together until the last year of his life. The love for Catherine, which, he said, had only been exceeded by the love of the saints, was replaced by a mellower emotion which coloured his later fiction, giving it a humour and lightness of touch which in his years with Catherine he had not experienced. And yet, for all the importance of women in Greene's life, his memorable characters are men; he never succeeded in portraying a woman as felt from within. As in the poetry of Donne, they remain the echoing chambers of the emotions of men.

The importance of sex in Greene's life, seemingly unrelated to his feelings for his children, or to other members of his family of the next generation, is constantly shadowed by his loneliness, his need for privacy, and his moods of deep blackness. What was life-affirming in sexuality was matched on his dark side by depression and contemplation of suicide. The story of his playing Russian roulette in his youth was often mentioned by Greene; and Shelden's contention that he used only a starter's pistol with blanks, while reflecting a more general view that the master storyteller knew how to invent to keep himself in the public eye, does not undercut a more important truth that Greene often lived close to the worst of all sins, despair.

> Despair is the price one pays for setting oneself an impossible aim. It is, one is told, the unforgiveable sin, but it is a sin the corrupt or evil man never practises. He always has hope. He never reaches the freezing-point of knowing absolute failure. Only the man of goodwill carries always in his heart this capacity for damnation. (HM 60)

As an artist, he was not alone in finding that success only intensified a sense of failure. His books sold more than twenty million copies, and were translated into forty languages. He was able to live wherever he wanted, in Paris, Capri, the French Riviera. Nevertheless, 'at the height of his fame as a writer, and at the height of his grand passion for Lady Walston, he was suicidal. Sometimes he set the date for death, saving up his sleeping pills [as Scobie in *The Heart of the Matter* does] because he wanted a termination point for his unhappiness.'[9] He once remarked that he was never particularly in love with life; his despair existed beyond success. This melancholy and unhappiness permeates much of his writing. Just as 'mad' Ireland hurt Yeats into poetry, so Greene's writing was born of, and sustained by, his unhappiness. While he rejected the absurdist view of the universe, he could not free himself from a terrible paradox that '*if* there be a God, *since* there is a God, the human race is implicated in some terrible aboriginal calamity'. Greene was here quoting Cardinal Newman in the epigraph to *The Lawless Roads* (1939); but this sense of a catastrophe in which all mankind is involved, incapable of resolution or amendment by individual or common demeanour, symbolizes much which the twentieth century has repeatedly proved. Greene found a qualified consolation in the premiss from which he begins; but that premiss cannot qualify or amend the facts of history. Greene's fiction reflects this and in doing so gives his writing a tone representative of the times through which he lived. He was perhaps also not so unusual, even in increasingly secular and material times, in expressing his basic outlook like this: 'The trouble is I don't believe my unbelief.'[10]

The divided self expressed in this sentence fractures in many more ways in Greene the novelist. Politically, his sympathies always remained with the dispossessed; and like Dostoevsky, with whom he has much in common in temperament if not in style, he preferred to write about them. The lieutenant and the whisky priest in *The Power and the Glory* are the subject of his fiction, not their political masters. 'That was the difference, he had always known, between his faith and theirs, the political leaders of the people who cared only for things like the state, the republic; this child was more important than a whole continent' (*PG* 82). What he saw as corruption in the exercise of power interested him in its victims as a metaphor for the individual in the human condition. Most of the time his characters embody his own awareness that we live alone and die alone; and in this solitariness, which no one can alleviate, he also expressed what the twentieth century has come to recognize as the fear in the

9

eternal silences of the universe. 'Loneliness is not shared with another – it is multiplied'.[11]

Greene's warning to his biographers about his self-concealment was justified. The contradictions in his attitudes, beliefs, and loyalties remain unresolved, bearing witness to the view he once expressed that we can never know another person. But these very contradictions, obsessions, and prejudices are themselves evidence of the divisions of self and allegiance which permeate Greene's times. Without them he could not have reflected as artist what was changing, ambivalent, and demanding in the world around him. As he himself said, 'we are at the heart of the disorder';[12] and his gift lay in the precision and lucidity with which he expressed it. Greene's alertness, apparent in his life and in his art, made him concerned with things that mattered in his time.

2

Travel, Dreams, and Films

> It can be a comfort sometimes to know that there is a world which is purely one's own – the experience in that world, of travel, danger, happiness, is shared with no one else. There are no witnesses. No libel actions. The characters I meet there have no memory of meeting me, no journalist or would-be biographer can check my account with another's. (*WO*, p. xvii)

Graham Greene began his last and posthumously published dream diary, *A World of my Own*, with these words; and he chooses the word 'travel' to characterize the entirely private world of dreams. In his waking life, as in his subconscious and creative lives, travel exercised a controlling influence. He greatly admired the novels of Trollope; but Greene could never have become the kind of novelist he was, if he had lived Trollope's life. The increase in the possibility of travel, and its practice, may yet turn out to be among the most culturally significant changes within the twentieth century, which in the twenty-first may again be superseded by the exchange of information on computerized highways. But that inability to be still in one's own room to which Pascal ascribed half the ills of mankind gives to Greene's life and work a restless anxiety, seen in its best light as an ongoing quest, and in its more doubtful form as a solitary man's need to remain in the limelight. (As a novelist committed to a life of action, he has much in common with his French contemporary, André Malraux.) The price paid by the traveller is an absence of peace, whether in mind or body, and a longing for home which can never be satisfied except for a brief reprieve. The word 'peace' recurs often in Greene's fiction and never more tellingly or ambivalently than in *The Heart of the Matter*. 'He [Scobie] dreamed of peace by day and night. Once in sleep it appeared to him as the great glowing shoulder of the moon heaving across his window like an iceberg,

Arctic and destructive in the moment before the world was struck... Peace seemed to him the most beautiful word in the language' (*HM* 60). To the writer who described his theme as rootlessness, and who only found home where he happened to be, peace remained elusive. Even writing becomes a 'form of action'.[1]

As with all lives, Greene's temperament and attitudes are deeply influenced by the time of his birth, his background, and his upbringing. When the British Empire still encompassed two-thirds of the world, a young man of Greene's background, educated in a public school and at Oxford, could still see his Englishness as a passport to adventure in many places. He belonged to a generation, brought up on adventure stories, who had missed the enormous disillusionment of the First World War, and who went out looking for adventure. 'In those days young writers made that sort of rather dangerous journey. Perhaps it was a way of proving oneself.'[2] His contemporaries, Evelyn Waugh and Peter Fleming, were among those who followed the same course. But Greene alone sustained it throughout his life. 'My subject is rootlessness – but then my subject matter is my life, so there's no paradox. The other day a critic suggested that I could not feel at home anywhere as I was forever globe-trotting. I replied that in fact I feel at home wherever I am.'[3]

As a boy he was enthralled by writers such as G. A. Henty, Stanley Weyman, and Rider Haggard in *King Solomon's Mines* who romanticized this way of living in the high noon of Empire. Wherever he went he took, as those heroes of Victorian fiction did, his Englishness with him. Although his novels were set in many different countries, his attitudes and his beliefs were, like those of his contemporaries, Eurocentric. When he wrote, '*We* are at the heart of the disorder' (emphasis added),[4] he expressed this 'prejudice'. In spite of the decline of the West, he saw no ideas which could guide the world to greater advantage than those which derived from it. Perhaps for this reason he never succeeded in bringing characters from other cultures to life. The Syrian Yusuf, like the Annamite Phuong, were imagined as figures from other cultures, not characters felt from within.

The Englishness which Greene took with him, formed from a love of adventure, literary and actual, shaped his style as well as his outlook. 'If you excite your audience first, you can put over what you will of horror, suffering, truth.'[5] Although he was dedicated to the craft of writing, assiduous in establishing a point of view in the narrative, and took increasing pains with his corrections as his career progressed (he wrote a novel in nine months at the outset, and took at least three years later on), he did not make important contributions to fictional form. His skills lay in the originality of his story-telling and his preoccupation with his characters. 'A novel is a work in which characters interrelate.'[6] His precision in depicting this depended on the establishment of an 'atmosphere'. His obsessions were projected onto the countries where he travelled; and his travels fed his obsessions. His self-assurance in his English identity made this possible.

Greene first travelled outside Europe in 1935, when he went with his cousin Barbara to Liberia in West Africa. His account was published in 1936 as *Journey without Maps*. The book was first called 'journey in the dark'; and, for the boy who had always been severely frightened by the dark, it was a significant title, which recognized the coincidence of unconscious fears and actual travelling. 'Freud', he observed, 'has made us conscious as we have never been before of those ancestral threads which still exist in our unconscious minds to lead us back.' (*JM* 295). But this first journey to Africa was to lead forward as well, and have repercussions throughout his life. He loved Africa with an intensity shared only by his love for Catherine Walston, and in writing to her he compared the two.

> I have loved no part of the world like this and I have loved no woman as I love you. You're my human Africa. I love your smell as I love these smells. I love your dark bush as I love the bush here, you change with the light as this place does, so that one all the time is loving something different and yet the same. I want to spill myself out into you as I want to die here.[7]

The love of Africa was to lead him back during the war, enabling him to write *The Heart of the Matter*. Later he was to go to Kenya during the Mau Mau troubles, and the Congo, about which he wrote *A Burnt Out Case* (1961). It was while travelling in the Cameroons that he was to meet the last love of his life, Yvonne Cloetta. He called that first visit to Liberia a 'trip which altered life'.[3]

Africa was important in another way too. It sharpened his sense of location: his eye for observed detail, too often spoiled in the early work by unnecessary or florid comparison, hardened under

13

the discipline of describing as a traveller what he saw, and analysing its psychological value for him. Up until 1936 his fiction had been set in England or Europe; Greene's London in *It's a Battlefield* (1934) owed much to Conrad's *The Secret Agent*, as had his first novel, *The Man Within* (1929). His next successful novel, *Stamboul Train* (1932), while showing again his sharp eye for rural and urban landscape, owed its atmosphere to the train and its travellers, who included, much to the disgust of some of his book-club readers, a pair of Lesbian lovers. *Stamboul Train* belongs to the tradition of adventure stories in exotic settings where characters, imprisoned together in a train or a ship, are pursuing their various ends, or being pursued. Liberia, by enabling him to see the contrast between England and Africa, confirmed his dislike of what he called the 'Headquarters of Empire' (later directed towards American economic imperialism) and at the same time drew him towards the 'inexplicable', which this other culture seemed to suggest, by asking where human civilization had gone astray. His 'journey without maps' taught him more keenly how difficult maps were to draw, how frontiers were not always visible (a moral as well as a geographical lesson), and strengthened his desire to be precise in attempting to draw them. From then on simplicity and precision became increasingly the stylistic aims he set for himself.

Greene's restlessness remained essential to the development of his art; but the places in which he spent time (even trouble spots) did not always result in a novel – for example, Malaya (during the war with the Communists) and Kenya (during the Mau Mau troubles). While his response to local atmosphere and landscape served to change the focus of his novels, travelling also remained important to their structure and content. Journeys, as in *The Power and the Glory*, are made necessary by the theme of pursuit, or escape, as in *The Human Factor* (1978). Travelling for pleasure (and escape!) provides the structure of *Travels with my Aunt* (1969) and *Monsignor Quixote*.

A journey into enemy territory affords a scene of the highest tension in *The Quiet American* (1955); while in *The End of the Affair* journeys back and forth across Clapham Common order a narrative of adulterous love. But, as he himself said, he did not travel in search of landscapes: 'I'm not interested in landscape, or how a house may be decorated – whether it contains a lamp or a staircase – except in so far as these things affect the evolution of any of the characters in the novel. That is why I am not a great admirer of Sir Walter Scott.'[9]

Greene could not have written his novels without the countries he travelled to; or without his travelling in the wide range of his reading. At the time of his death his library contained more than 3,000 volumes, many of them annotated in detail. As his conversations with Fr Duran revealed, his literary tastes were eclectic, and sharply personal. In his fiction, his absorption of books was crucial in forming his style. His carefully chosen epigraphs for each novel attest to his knowledge; his characters quote and are often well read; but these allusions are never drawn in – as, for example, in the novels of Aldous Huxley – to display erudition; they fall naturally, if noticed at all, within the scope of ordinary human discourse.

His private travelling in the world of dreams was no less important. Who knows, he said, whether what we write when we are awake is the same as what we write in the mind where we are asleep. Some dreams enabled him to overcome a 'blockage'; others provided him with material for short stories or even an idea for a new novel (as with It's a Battlefield and The Honorary Consul). In writing A Burnt-Out Case, he attributed a dream of his own to Querry, and so succeeded in resolving the impasse he had reached in writing the novel. Conscious and subconscious processes were deeply integrated in his creativity.

As a very private man, Greene seldom lectured; but on one occasion he related how a dream had given him his theory of the common evolution of God and Man, and the common identity of God and Satan. This dream was used in The Honorary Consul.

> The God I believe in must be responsible for all the evil as well as for all the saints. He has to be a God made in our image with a night-side as well as a day-side. When you speak of the horror, Eduardo, you are speaking of the night-side of God. I believe the time will come when the night-side will wither away, like your communist state, Aquino, and we shall see only the simple daylight of the good God. You believe in evolution, Eduardo, even though sometimes whole generations of men slip backwards to the beasts. It is a long struggle and a long suffering evolution, and I believe God is suffering the same evolution that we are, but perhaps with more pain. (HC 225–6)

In The Comedians (1966) four or five of Brown's dreams play an essential part in the novel. 'I call them dreams of grace, for poor Brown is saved through these dreams.'[10] As often happens with Greene, the personal and the literary coalesce in this admission, with its debt to Dostoevsky.

Dreams, travel, and boyhood reading come together in a passage from *The Human Factor* (1978) which also says much about Greene's method of composition.

> He didn't want to sleep until he was sure from her breathing that Sarah was asleep first. Then he allowed himself to strike, like his childhood hero Allan Quartermain, on that long slow underground stream which bore him on towards the interior of the dark continent where he hoped that he might make a permanent home, in a city where he could be accepted as a citizen, as a citizen without any pledge of faith, not the City of God or Marx, but the city called peace of Mind. (*HF* 107)

All three are fused here in a passage which culminates in an unresolved anxiety, characteristic of Greene.

'Under the Garden', a short story which first appeared in *A Sense of Reality* (1963), offers an allegorical account of the relation between the unconscious (what is underground), childhood experience, and journeys of exploration. It also illustrates that element of fantasy which Greene used from time to time in his narratives, and which matures in his late novel *Dr Fischer of Geneva, or the Bomb Party* (1980). In both of them he tamed his nightmares by using them as background.[11]

Wilditch, a middle-aged man and a great traveller, whose life is threatened by a lung condition, returns to Winton Hall, a house which he had known as a boy, and about which he has written a story for the school magazine. (Winton Hall is based on Harston House, which Greene often visited in his youth, and which he used in a number of novels, as well as the play, *The Potting Shed* (1958).) Picking this story up after forty years, Wilditch is irritated by the distortions of an actual dream which he still recalls, and which he now decides to write down. 'It could have been nothing else but a dream, but a dream too was an experience, the images of a dream had their own integrity, and he felt professional anger at this false report...' (*CS* 182). He dreamed of crossing a lake to an island, both greatly increased in size from those in the garden of Winton. In dreams, as he says, a puddle can contain a continent. He gets lost on the island at nightfall, but he feels no fear. 'It was as though even at seven I was accustomed to travel. All the rough journeys of the future were already in me then, like a muscle which had only to develop.' (*SR* 184). Fantasies, originating in dreams, provide the makings of fiction, as well as dreams *tout court*.

The boy finds a tunnel underground, leading to a cave where a filthy old man lives. His bed is a pile of potato sacks, and his chair a lavatory seat. The old man, who goes by the name of Javitt, offers the boy subversive advice on sex, on authority ('be disloyal'), and on the need to survive on his own.

When Wilditch has finished writing down his dream, he goes downstairs to meet the old gardener, Ernest, who at once reminds him of Javitt. The story he wrote as a boy was created out of a fantasy about the garden, and the gardener. The 'true' tale which he writes as an older man involves an unscrambling of this childhood experience, in which dream, fantasy, and reality were mixed up.

'Under the Garden' says a great deal about Greene's creative imagination, and more generally about the nature of fictional truth, based on transformation and often evasion. In *The Honorary Consul*, the novelist, Dr Saavedra, attempting to write a letter about Charley Fortnum, complains: 'In a novel I could have created him in a few sentences. It is his reality which defeats me. I am hamstrung by his reality. When I write down a phrase it is as though Fortnum himself put a hand on my wrist and said, "But this is not how I am at all"' (*HC* 155). In *Monsignor Quixote*, he will use this problem as a comic device, by making his priest, to the intense irritation of his Bishop, claim descent from a fictional character. Greene, it is clear, knew his Pirandello.

Shit and excrement figure prominently in the conversation of the foul old man under the garden. His treasure, when it is rediscovered, will turn out to be a chamber-pot. The underground place is no 'locus amoenus'. Here, as often, Greene's obsessions are being reworked in different locations and with different narrative ends. The allegorical and symbolic narrative in 'Under the Garden' reworks material used earlier in the climax to Greene's film script for Carol Reed's *The Third Man* (1950). And this tale, too, has more than a little allegorical truth in its relation to Greene's life.

Holly Martins (Joseph Cotten, who played the part in the film, objected to the original name of Rollo) is a writer, invited to Vienna by his schoolboy friend Harry Lime. He arrives in time for his funeral, and his suspicion about the circumstances of Lime's death leads to his discovery that Lime has faked his own death in order to avoid arrest for trading in fake penicillin. The pursuit of friendship leads, in the climax of the film, to the Viennese sewers, a place where death waits, and friendship ends in murder. What lies in the unconscious offers no comfort.

The Third Man is also a memorable depiction of post-war Europe, where the black market affords rich pickings to those without social conscience, and where the sewers enable a man to move between the Allied and Russian zones of Vienna. A story of pursuit and detection becomes also a question of identity. Who is the third man? The answer to that question involves an underground traverse of zones which the mind normally separates, a breaking-down of compartments which are involved in self-preservation.

Films, like dreams, are composed of images which editing joins in a visual narrative. Carol Reed perceived how cinematic Greene's imagination was. He succeeded in filming Greene's work as no other director did, because he shot the fusion of dream and reality. The light which first shines on Harry Lime's face as he stands in a doorway, and reveals the living dead to Holly, is a moment from nightmare, where, as Greene said, no defences exist. It is also the moment when Holly has to confront for the first time how things really are: Lime is a wanted man on the run.

Before *The Third Man* Greene had already collaborated with Carol Reed on another memorable film, *The Fallen Idol*, based on a story he had written in 1935 called 'The Basement Room'; but, in spite of the fusion of their talents, Greene admitted the relief with which he went back to 'the one-man business, to the privacy of a room in which I bear the full responsibility for failure'.[12] In his creative life, Greene had more than a little in common with the wanted man on the run.

When Greene was asked if he felt that his narrative style had been influenced by script-writing for the screen, he replied it had not, but that his style had been influenced by going to the cinema. The montage effects in the fiction, the long tracking shots, as, for example, in following Scobie at the start of *The Heart of the Matter*, have often been remarked on. But the cinema was important for

Greene in another way. Between 1935 and 1940 he reviewed films – more than 400 of them – for the *Spectator* and *Night and Day*. His film reviews, like Shaw's theatre and music criticism, compelled him to crystallize his own attitudes, to develop in the broadest sense an aesthetic. They express his likes, and his dislikes, as an artist, and show where his sympathies, and antipathies, lie, in matters of style and content. Like T. S. Eliot in his essays, Greene was clearing an area in which his own art was nourished. Plot matters only as a dramatized illustration of a character in a way of life. He admires and notes the director who has an eye for detail which expresses human relationships; he approves of what he sees as 'moral realism'; and he deplores what he sees in American films like *The Road Back*.

> What it really emphasizes is the eternal adolescence of the American mind, to which literature means the poetry of Longfellow and morality means keeping Mother's Day and looking after the kid sister's purity. One came daunted out of the cinema, and there, strolling up the Haymarket, were the American Legionaries, arm in arm with women dressed just the same – all guide-books, glasses, and military salutes: caps marked Santa Anna and Minnesota: hair – what there was of it – grey, but the same adolescent features, plump, smug, sentimental, ready for the easy tear and the hearty laugh and the fraternity yell. What use in pretending that with these allies it was ever possible to fight for civilisation? (*PD* 172–3)

Greene wrote this in October 1937; four years later we would be fighting with them precisely for civilization. But what emerged after the war, continued to affront Greene morally and aesthetically, as US economic expansion spread round the globe. These views shaped by his experience of American films dominated the last phase of his writing, and his involvement in South and Central American politics.

What he liked and admired is no less apparent in these film reviews, and corresponds to his own early division of his work into novels and entertainments. René Clair, Ernst Lubitsch, and Frank Capra were admired for their sense of the human comedy, for qualities such as lightness and charm, and their ability to show how innocence is preserved, and a good man survives in a bad world. Capra's *Mr Deeds Goes to Town*, about a young provincial who inherits twenty million dollars from an uncle he has never seen, and who learns the hard way the social consequences of

19

being wealthy, especially appealed to him. Goodness, simplicity, disinterestedness are the qualities of Mr Deeds; and they also touch works as different as *Our Man in Havana, Travels with my Aunt,* and *Monsignor Quixote.*

The two greatest film directors, according to Greene, were Fritz Lang and Jean Duvivier. In the work of both of them he picks out qualities which characterize his own best work; the refusal of sentimental endings (for example, *Brighton Rock*) and narratives which involve 'the freedom-loving human spirit trapped and pulling at the chain' (*PD* 144). In reviewing Duvivier's *Un carnet de bal,* he wrote:

> In one episode we have Duvivier's real greatness – the seedy doctor at Marseilles so used to furtive visitors and illegal operations that he doesn't wait for questions before he lights the spirit flame; the dreadful cataracted eye; the ingrained dirt upon his hands; the shrewish wife picked up on God-knows what low music-hall railing behind bead curtains: the continuous shriek and grind of winch and crane. Nostalgia, sentiment, regret; the padded and opulent emotions wither before the evil detail; the camera shoots at a slant so that the dingy flat rears like a sinking ship ... The genuine poverty is in Duvivier's Marseilles flat – the tin surgical basin, the antiseptic soap, the mechanical illegality and the complete degradation. (*PD* 184)

As a territory, and in its detail, this corresponds closely to Greene's moral and spiritual obsessions.

In watching these films, Greene's eye as an artist was always alert to the craft which went into their making; and many of his judgements have survived the test of time. He appreciated equally the realism of William Wyler, and the poetry of Bunuel. These qualities in his writing were nourished through the art of the cinema. In the following sentence from *The Quiet American* the camera in close-up becomes the eye of the traveller and the mind of the dreamer, illustrating once more how fertile a relationship existed in his art between travel, dreams, and films. 'She nodded and taking up the needle again began to heat the opium. That night I woke from one of those short deep opium sleeps, ten minutes long, that seem a whole night's rest ... (*QW* 22).

3

'A writer who happens to be a Catholic'

Greene disliked being described as a Catholic writer. None the less, his name became known around the world as the author of *The Power and the Glory*, and even more *The Heart of the Matter*, novels in which his obsession with the problems of being a Catholic are at the centre of the narrative. From the size of his readership, and the controversy his novels caused outside and inside the Catholic Church, Greene's writing clearly touched on issues which seemed important and pressing at the time they were written. These novels continue to be the ones most generally admired, even by critics, like Michael Shelden, who are hostile to Greene and his reputation. The appeal of literature has never been dependent on the assumption of shared beliefs between writer and reader: the power to excite, interest, and challenge through the quality of the writing, the vibrancy of the language, matter more. None the less, Greene's position at the close of the twentieth century continues to raise problems of response which need to be discussed. As a Catholic writer in his period, he is far from being alone: Bernanos, Claudel, Mauriac remain figures of indisputable importance in France – a prominence shared by Evelyn Waugh, Muriel Spark, and Graham Greene in England. In this chapter I shall concentrate less on the doctrinal issues – brilliantly discussed by Roger Sharrock in his book *Saints, Sinners and Comedians* (1984) – than on the perspectives which give Greene's preoccupations their cultural significance.

Greene's first major Catholic novel was *Brighton Rock*. In writing about it, Greene admitted that he began to use Catholic characters because he wanted 'to examine more closely the effect of faith on action' (*WE* 59). In 1937 the problem for 'Christian' Europe was also beginning to express itself in stark terms. To what extent did 1,900 years of Christianity provide any kind of defence against the evil in Nazi Germany. These were problems which the writer could not avoid – particularly a writer like Greene, who saw writing as a form of action, and who, influenced by Henry James, recognized the problem of evil in human nature as central to the religious sense on which, he believed, art depended. Pinkie is not a symbolic figure, but he is a representative figure; and the Brighton which Greene describes belongs more to an 'imaginary geographic region' than to the actual town. 'I had every intention of describing it, but it was as though my characters had taken the Brighton I knew into their own consciousness and transformed the whole picture (I have never again felt so much the victim of my inventions)' (*WE* 62). What the novel reveals more potently than any of Greene's subsequent works is the ineffectiveness of faith in acting as a brake upon evil. While the novel finally turns on a doctrinal matter as to whether there is any limit to the mercy of God, its central fascination lies with that far wider question for Catholic Europe of the 1930s as to how the evil in human nature was to be resisted. In many of his later novels Greene gives his narrative a very broad canvas – Mexico, West Africa, Vietnam; here the confinement to particular parts of a single town sharpens the intensity through the narrowness of the focus. Here ills may be done, and not heard of again, as the epigraph to *Brighton Rock* indicates. But national diseases are born of such local ills.

It is noticeable, though not surprising, for a writer to whom the religious sense was inseparable from art, how frequently Greene quotes from, or refers to, writers of the seventeenth century. (His one biography was also about the seventeenth-century poet Lord Rochester). But he preferred the plays of Webster to those of Shakespeare. Returning in many novels to the emotion of hate, he often shows a temperamental affinity with the Jacobean dramatists who saw hate as leading to damnation. Greene's description of Pinkie, the boy gangster, recalls the characterization of a Flamineo or a Bosola in Webster's plays (while wittily inverting Words-worth's 'Immortality Ode').

> There was poison in his veins, though he grinned and bore it. He had been insulted. He was going to show the world. They thought because he was only seventeen...he jerked his narrow shoulders back at the memory that he'd killed his man, and these bogies who thought they

were clever weren't clever enough to discover that. He trailed the clouds of his own glory after him: hell lay about him in his infancy. He was ready for more deaths. (*BR* 68)

Later he will ask in fury, 'must I massacre the whole world?' Damnation, and the flames of hell, as a punishment, torments Pinkie's mind, but never restrains his action.

The novel is rightly seen by many critics as a detective story. Ida Arnold is determined to pursue the killer of Fred Hale, because she believes in right and wrong, and wants Justice to be done. Ida Arnold's doggedness would have resulted in Pinkie's arrest, if he had not died by falling over the cliff, after being disfigured with his own vitriol. This secular narrative is fused with the metaphysical detective story in which God will be both sleuth and judge. As the priest tells Rose at the end, 'You can't conceive, my child, nor can I or anyone – the...appalling...strangeness of the mercy of God' (*BR* 246). But between these two narratives of solved and unsolved detection there runs another of social implication, the hell which lay about Pinkie in his infancy. Rose asks him: 'Nelson Place. Do you know it?'

> 'Oh, I've passed through,' he said airily, but he could have drawn its plan on the turf as accurately as a surveyor: the barred and battlemented Salvation Army gaff at the corner, his own home beyond in Paradise Place, the houses which looked as though they had passed through an intensive bombardment, flapping gutters and glassless windows, an iron bedstead rusting in a front garden, the smashed and wasted ground in front where houses had been pulled down for model flats which had never gone up.' (*BR* 90)

The court in which Pinkie briefly rules through fear is a place in which the poison courses through houses rotten with poverty and neglect. Here, in moment of crisis, faith never acts as a brake upon action. Greene's success in creating the inwardness of Pinkie shows that at such moments it is simply absent, except as a faint nostalgia, as if for something he had lost or forgotten or rejected.

> 'Good God,' Mr Prewitt said, 'how did it happen?'
> The Boy said: 'These stairs have needed mending a long while. I've told Billy about it, but you can't make the bastard spend money.' (*BR* 123)

None the less, as Prewitt points out, the rotten wood lies on top of Spicer's body, proclaiming the murder. Evil thrives too on social deprivation and exclusion, as it had in Hitler's rise to power.

Pinkie and Rose, the girl he marries in a secular ceremony to ensure that she cannot testify against him, and whom he nearly persuades to kill herself, confess their Catholicism to each other early in the novel. It gives them a powerful fear of Hell; and to Rose, however faintly, a hope of Heaven; but their actions are determined by a world of extreme poverty, murder, violence, and joyless copulation. The question raised by the novel is not so much whether mercy is to be found, as in the famous quotation, between the stirrup and the ground; but rather the inoperancy of faith to restrain evil, even in the face of the flames of Hell – perhaps the most important question which faced Catholic Europe in the 1930s. Albert Camus, writing in 1948, still saw it as the great failure of the Catholic Church in the period of Fascism that its voice was not more clearly heard. 'For a long time during those frightful years I waited for a great voice to speak up in Rome. I, an unbeliever? Precisely. For I knew that the spirit would be lost if it did not utter a cry of condemnation when faced with force.'[1] In Pinkie, Greene mirrors the inoperancy of faith against evil.

The fourth of Greene's major Catholic novels, *The End of the Affair*, is also set in England, this time in London. I want to consider it before turning to the two novels of broader canvas, set in Mexico and West Africa, because in some ways it forms a companion to *Brighton Rock*. Faith, instead of being impotent to restrain evil, becomes the cause of hate.

Sarah, the lover of a middle-aged writer, Maurice Bendrix, believes him to have been killed in an air raid. When he recovers consciousness, and goes back upstairs to their bedroom, he finds her on her knees praying to anything that existed to restore him to life; the bargain that she strikes with God being that, if this happens, she will give him up as her lover, and return to her husband, Henry. She does this, while attempting to prove the absurdity of her vow by visiting a rationalist teacher; his secular outlook only pushes her deeper into the faith she is trying to avoid. Baptized as a Catholic at the age of 2, she has once again caught faith like an infection or a disease (her mother in having her baptized hoped that the innoculation would take). After her death, caused by taking a walk in the cold for the purpose of avoiding Bendrix, she is associated with two miraculous cures: the appendicitis of Parkis's boy, and the urticaria on the face of the rationalist teacher who has inadvertently drawn her back to the Church. But the novel is less concerned, and less effectively involved, with these miracles than with the hate which God's removal of Sarah from human sexual love arouses in Bendrix. The word 'hate' recurs six times in the second paragraph of the novel, and will dominate the text, like a black thumb-print, till its climax, in Bendix's final litany: 'I wanted Sarah for a life-time and You took her away. With Your great schemes You ruin our happiness like a harvester ruins a mouse's nest: I hate You, God, I hate You as though You existed' (*EA* 191). The hypothetical and self-contradictory nature of the assertion dramatizes a general human predicament as well as a theological paradox. Arthur Miller in *Incident in Vichy* (1965) wrote of the human need for a Jew to hate: 'Jew is only the name we give to that stranger, that agony we cannot feel, that death we look at like a cold abstraction. Each man has his Jew; it is the other.'[2] In *The End of the Affair* hate, like love, is seen as a secretion which fixes upon some object, whether real or imagined, and identifies that object as the sole impediment to happiness and fulfilment. Bendrix complains to God, 'I wanted something very simple and very easy.' Sarah's withdrawal into faith, and her struggle to maintain the vow made in the air raid, is seen as an act which destroys the possibility of Bendrix achieving those goals. His narrative explores the complexities of an emotion which courses through every level of social and political life. While the novel is ostensibly concerned with God's responsibility for his creation, its wider human application is also apparent. As W. H. Auden wrote in a famously amended line, 'We must love one another, or die'.[3] The obstacles to that flow not only from the problems of faith, but from the human need to identify 'a Jew'.

The End of the Affair, which Greene began in 1948, would not have been written if he had not started his intense relationship with Catherine Walston the previous year. The novel reflects in the character of Bendrix the tormented jealousy and insecurity Greene suffered in this affair, which was to continue intermittently until 1961. The novel is dedicated 'to C'; and its epigraph from Léon Bloy draws attention to a major theme in the novel which its theological and secular critics have often missed: 'Man has places in his heart which do not yet exist, and into them enters suffering in order that they may have existence.' This can be read as a Christian justification of suffering; but, in the context of the novel, its implications are somewhat different. The affair begins in 1939 only because Bendrix wants to find out about the life of a civil servant for the novel he is writing (Greene, the writer, described himself as a man with a splinter of ice in his heart); but the desire to get copy turns him into a writer of a very different kind, with the need to mine and articulate those extremities of feeling dominated by love, hate, and jealousy; the first and last have little place in *Brighton Rock*.

Through the inclusion of Sarah's journal, Greene breaks up the first-person narrative with its inevitable distortions and special pleading, and includes a different kind of emotion to which the final sentence of the whole novel returns: a longing for release from the intensities of emotion itself, and a freedom from the lacerations, whether of self or others, to which they lead. Sarah, able to live for the moment as Bendrix cannot, seems at times innoculated against remorse and despondency; but she longs for freedom, escape from his unwillingness to believe that she loves him, of which he demands constant proof. 'Two days ago,' she writes in her journal for 12 February 1946, 'I had such a sense of peace and quiet and love. Life was going to be happy again...' (*EA* 123). Then she dreams of Bendrix, and when she wakes up, it is to the old sense of weariness and pain, and a desire for ordinary corrupt human love which involves drinking in a bar, or eating sandwiches together. As she admits in her final letter to him, where she once again reaffirms that she will not go away with him, she admits that she wants to have her cake and eat it; and the result is a wholly new kind of pain. And now she has no fight left. 'I pray to God He won't keep me alive like this' (*EA* 147). This emotional and spiritual exhaustion in Sarah is reflected at the end of the novel in Bendrix's own expense of spirit. 'Oh God, You've done enough, You've robbed me of enough, I'm too tired and old to learn to love, leave me alone for ever' (*EA* 192). The skill of Bendrix's narration in its movement backwards and forwards in time, so that the reader never loses sight of the complex ebbs and tides of feeling, is matched by its enquiry into emotions which neither mind nor body is capable of sustaining, and which at the outset had no existence. Few modern novels are so skilful or so relentless within a narrow compass in showing that frontier which exists between emotional exhaustion and a suicidal despair.

The longing for release from desire and for peace of mind reflects Greene's understanding of the anguish in contemporary secular and materialist culture, and has a generality of reference outside the Catholic imagination. In *The Power and the Glory* and *The Heart of the Matter* these themes are also present, but here Greene sets them in the larger context of social and political conflict in Mexico and West Africa. *Brighton Rock* and *The End of the Affair* centre upon the intense emotions of a single character; in these other novels Greene's imagination is drawn to wider cultural issues, as well as to a sharper focus on the sacramental nature of the Catholic religion, and the operation of grace.

Greene visited Mexico for five weeks in 1938 to investigate the persecution of the Catholics which had begun under President Calles in 1926, and had led to the execution of priests who did not go into hiding, or renounce their faith. The people too, he was told, died like dogs. 'I hate this country and its people,' he was to write.[4] This was reflected in *The Lawless Roads*, the factual account he wrote of his travels. The villages he visited, the journey he made by mule, his sufferings from illness and the climate, were used soon after in *The Power and the Glory*. But Mexico was equally important in terms of its metaphysical influence on him. It gave an emotional expression to the intellectual faith he had adopted before his marriage to Vivien Dayrell-Browning. It also confirmed a sense of some 'aboriginal calamity' which had befallen the world, and where 'either there is no Creator, or this living society of men is in a true sense discarded from his presence...' (*LR*, Epigraph). Mexico confronted him with the dilemma of the choice between his faith, which depended on a sense of 'inexplicable goodness', and this country, which symbolized a 'deus absconditus'. His intense dislike of Mexico, physically and politically, was tempered only by his perception that so many years had passed in England 'since the war between faith and anarchy: we live in an ugly indifference' (*LR* 26). In his dislike of indifference he was close in spirit to those seventeenth-century poets in whom metaphysical and sexual anxiety were fused by a passionate intellect. *The Power and the Glory* resolves this tension in a narrative about faith sustained by a fine and imperishable thread.

Greene's whisky priest (unnamed like the lieutenant who hunts him down) is described as a 'small man dressed in a shabby black suit'. When executed at the end of the novel, he is reduced to

27

'something unimportant which had to be cleared away'. The reduction of the human to the inanimate has been paralleled in the novel by the priest's growing recognition of how little he can do, without even the wine to celebrate the Mass. His inner life must be lived on the edge of despair (the unforgivable sin); and his physical life on the edge of extinction. Greene's interest lies on the narrow line which the life of the whisky priest traces between these two forms of annihilation; and more specifically in the form of continuity which the whisky priest embodies. He is the last of the priests in the district; and in his wandering he brings what consolation he can to those he visits. After his execution, when the line seems broken, another priest appears: 'A stranger stood in the street, a tall pale thin man with a rather sour mouth, who carried a small suitcase...' (PG 221). The narrative opens as it began with the appearance of the priest who ensures the sacramental tradition is not extinguished. Catholicism in practice, like the political engagement of which Greene approves, is seen as a subversive activity, opposed equally to indifference and to repression.

But faith, however close to extinction, is relit elsewhere. In an address on the theme, 'Is Christian Civilisation in Peril?' (1948), Greene ended with a fantasy about the last Pope, wandering the world with the fear that what he believed eternal might die with him. To ensure that this happens, the World Dictator shoots him. 'At that instant, in the second between the pressure on the trigger and the skull cracking, a thought crossed the Dictator's mind: "Is it just possible that what this man believed in is true?" Another Christian had been born.'[5] Like his friend, Evelyn Waugh, who, at the close of *Brideshead Revisited*, has Charles Ryder see 'the small red flame... burning anew among the old stones', Greene is drawn to the idea that faith is always rekindled, however close it comes to being extinguished or forgotten. In this sober and imperilled conviction he adopts a cultural position which avoids fanaticism and dogmatism while allowing for a continuity which transcends a biological or humanist interpretation of things – a theme taken up in another great Catholic novel of the period, within a wholly different cultural context in Japan: Shusaku Endo's *Silence* (1967).

The influence of faith upon action, without effect in *Brighton Rock*, is seen as the determining force in *The Power and the Glory*. From the whisky priest's arrival at the port from which he might have made his escape, the narrative follows the journey on which his ministry is continued. At each place where he rests, his faith is tested anew, until he makes the final and fatal choice to hear the confession of the American murderer, ensuring his own arrest and execution. He knows himself to be a bad priest, who, as well as drinking, has fathered a child, and who lives in fear of the death to which he will have to be dragged, his legs not fully under control. With another part of him he desires eternal peace, but not until he can no longer be of use in saving a single soul. However deep his sense of abandonment in a dying cooling world, and his awareness of his own ineffectuality, he has to go on living; and that for the whisky priest means attempting wherever he can to administer the sacraments. In this respect the novel is specifically Catholic; but it dramatizes a more general allegory, of the frontier in the individual which cannot be abandoned. Arthur Miller in his 'Introduction' to his *Collected Plays* puts it like this: 'I take it that if one could know enough about a human being one could discover some conflict, some value, some challenge, however minor or major, which he cannot find it in himself to walk away from or turn his back on.'[6] Greene too is concerned with the point at which a man has to say no to preserve his sense of himself: ' "Renounce your faith," Coral Fellowes advises him. He said, "It's impossible. There's no way. I'm a priest. It's out of my power" ' (*PG* 40). However bad a priest, the whisky priest cannot change what he is, any more than the lieutenant can give up his quest to hunt him down, or the *mestizo* escape from the role of Judas, who will betray the priest for his pieces of silver. Identity for them is fixed and 'eternal'. Such power as each of them wields brings with it no glory. If such attributes are given by God, they remain shrouded in human ignorance: 'For Thine is the Kingdom...'.

The central narrative of *The Power and the Glory* re-enacts a myth of pursuit and betrayal. As an archetypal narrative, its roots are as much pagan as Christian; and its appeal popular and immediate, inviting anticipation of the end, and excitement in the lucky escape – most notably, when the lieutenant releases his victim from prison with a coin which is the price of a Mass (*PG* 140). But the archetypal story occurs within a narrative where characters are named (unlike the whisky priest and the lieutenant), and identities are fixed only by the locality in which they live. Home to Mr Tench, the dentist, means the four walls behind which one sleeps *and* the place to which one will retire. If the peso had not dropped, he would have gone home long since. Nevertheless, he still hopes: ' "I'll retire. Go home. Live as a gentleman ought to live. This" – he gestured at the bare base room – "I'll forget all this. Oh, it won't be long now. I'm an optimist" ' (*PG* 15). Nevertheless, at the end of the novel, he is still insisting: 'This time he was going to clear out, clear out for good' (*PG* 217). Escape remains a possibility for him, even if unrealized, as it does for Coral Fellowes. Both expatriates and Mexicans live their lives within the possibility of change, which is to say within the naturalistic tradition of which this part of the novel belongs. In spite of the brief time (or perhaps because of it) Greene spent in Mexico, his sense of various localities which the priest passes through on his journey is descriptive, not figurative, providing a naturalistic background for the central symbolic drama:

> There were signs of cultivation; stumps of trees and the ashes of fires where the ground was being cleared for a crop... A woman came out of a hut and watched him lagging up the path on a tired mule. The tiny village, not more than two dozen huts round a dusty plaza, was made to pattern, but it was a pattern which lay close to his heart. He felt secure... (*PG* 61).

Until the last qualification this is lifted from Greene's own experience, and might still be taken from the journal of a traveller to Central or South America. The sense of security, false as it turns out to be, belongs to the whisky priest alone, who knows he has come to a place where he can trust a woman not to betray him, and where he will see the child for whom he feels an overpowering love: 'This child was more important than a whole continent' (*PG* 82). The map of this abandoned land is transfigured here, as it will be later in another way when he reaches the homestead of the Lehrs and experiences a temporary peace. The description of Mexico, vital though it is, becomes the means of revealing the values of the interior life. When Coral Fellowes discovers in the banana store a lot of little crosses, she surmises: 'He must have lain down among the bananas and tried to relieve his fear by writing something, and this was all he could think of. The child stood in her woman's pain and looked at them: a horrible novelty enclosed her whole morning: it was as if today everything was memorable' (*PG* 54). Throughout the novel the memorable is inscribed, however tentatively, on the abandoned. The conflict of ideas, viewpoints, and perspectives which structure a culture also structures the novel. Most obviously this is true of the opposition between the lieutenant's outlook and the priest's. The lieutenant's is socially determined, fired by the zeal to eliminate for the next generation

> everything which had made him miserable, all that was poor, superstitious, and corrupt. They deserved nothing less than the truth – a vacant universe and a cooling world, the right to be happy in any way they chose. He was quite prepared to make a massacre for their sakes – first the Church and then the foreigner and then the politician – even his own chief would one day have to go. He wanted to begin the world again with them, in a desert. (PG 58).

The lieutenant in his desire to obliterate the Church has no compunction in shooting hostages as often as necessary to ensure the betrayal of his prey. Blood is the price of what he considers to be socially progressive and ameliorative. God, and His church, never do anything except make people tolerate poverty. As in the other great political novel of this period, Arthur Koestler's *Darkness at Noon* (1940), the question raised is whether the ends justify the means. For Koestler, ends cannot be separated from the human adequacy of the means to achieve them. For Greene, the interest lies in the beliefs aroused by the ends, and the emotions which inspire them. The lieutenant in his willingness to massacre is fired by hate; and hate is 'just a failure of imagination' (PG 131). The whisky priest, for all his weakness, does not suffer from such a failure, either in his love for his child or in his willingness to accept the inadequacy of human imagination in relation to the love of God; the taste of God's love is like the 'smallest glass of love mixed with a pint-pot of ditch-water. We wouldn't recognise *that* love' (PG 199–200). The priest can see that such love might even look like hate. No one is ever freed from the threat of this failure.

On a miniature scale, this drama of pain reflects the global purges of the twentieth century, where in the name of some ultimate and unrealized good, hate has inspired and justified massacres on an unprecedented scale. There, too, that failure of imagination which justifies hate also ensured their futility.

This ideological conflict between the priest and the lieutenant forms the centre of a pattern of oppositions in the narrative between loyalty and betrayal, hope and despair, success and failure, the desire for peace and the necessity for subversive activity. To believe in peace, whether before or after death, is a kind of heresy. In the province where the Lehrs exist, where confessions can be heard and masses celebrated without fear, the whisky priest discovers that he never really believed in this peace. He is called back, as Greene himself frequently was, to the active sector of the line where the peace so often dreamed of means no more than a dream when offered. In this combative attitude, there exists the perspective of the artist drawn to the rejection of the *status quo*, and the emotions of the man whose desire to love can never be reconciled with his capacity for hate. In this condition of continuing dissent, the only possible reconciliation comes from a power beyond human ignorance. 'I don't know how awful the human heart looks to Him. But I do know this – that if there's ever been a single man in this state damned, then I'll be damned too' (*PG* 200). The Justice of God is inseparable from His mercy to all sorts and conditions of men; and the instrument of His mercy the operation of grace.

In *The Heart of the Matter* the influence of faith on action becomes internalized: a matter of the salvation or damnation of the individual soul. The drama of the novel arises out of Scobie's relation to God, and to the two women whom in different ways he claims to love. He cannot, as a good Catholic, look after his own soul at whatever cost to another, because Scobie is also a good man. To use a phrase associated with Donne, his soul is in a state of clamour; and Scobie resolves his conflict in a way which Donne contemplated in *Biathanatos*, but did not pursue: suicide. The suicide of the young district officer, Pemberton, whose body Scobie goes up-country to identify, imprints itself on Scobie's imaginings, reducing his defences against the self-destructive impulse, which the fear of eternal damnation otherwise bolsters. As he confides in his wife, 'Pemberton's suicide upset me.' She reassures him: 'How silly, dear. Nothing like that could ever happen with us. We're Catholics' (*HM* 96).[7]

The skill of the novel exists in its probing of the gap between what belief enjoins and the emotional disorder with which it cannot hold discourse. The 'heart of the matter' turns out to be the disintegration of Scobie's personality under stresses he cannot resolve. His desire to think well of himself is gradually eroded by his loss of integrity as police-officer and husband.

Scobie is laughingly called 'Scobie the Just' by the Commissioner of Police, who compares him to Aristides, renowned for his honesty. This image of himself which Scobie attempts to sustain arouses in him a feeling of responsibility for the well-being of others which proves beyond his power to ensure. Scobie's Englishness, contrasted throughout the novel with Yusuf's Syrian temperament, combines moral integrity with destructive pride. Yusuf's attitude to women is that they have to accept the way in which men choose to behave: 'You say to each of them, "I do not care a damn. I sleep with whom I please. You take me or leave me. I do not care a damn." They always take you, Major Scobie.' (*HM* 241). Scobie wants to compensate his wife for the ways in which he feels he has failed her, and for the failure of his love for her, since the death of their only child three years previously in England. To that sense of loss has been added 'the tide of her melancholy, and disappointment' (*HM* 21), culminating in her bitterness at his failure to be appointed Commissioner of Police (ironically reversed at the end of the novel, when Scobie has passed the point of no return). Scobie feels guilt, responsibility, and pity for Louise. He borrows money from Yusuf, to finance Louise's vacation in South Africa, and so puts himself in the power of a man who wants the protection of the police. But Louise Scobie's discontents, which arouse her husband's pity, are not attributable only to his failings. They arise too out of the colonial way of life in West Africa during the Second World War. The novel has sometimes been criticized for its racialist tone. This is misguided. One of the strengths of the novel lies in its representation, through vocabulary and stance, of the racially determined nature of the society it portrays, where nothing is separable from the colonial context and the values created by it. The members of the ruling caste are estranged from those they govern, and alienated from each other by class and rank. Boredom and absurdity are added to the discomforts of the climate; and the loneliness this way of life engenders. In every day only a few moments of compensation exist. 'In the evening the port became beautiful for perhaps five minutes. The laterite roads that were so ugly and clay-heavy by day became a delicate flower-like pink. It was the hour of content' (*HM* 26). Scobie at least has this; but 'literary Louise' as she is jokingly known at the club, with its characteristically Philistine conversation, finds refuge only in poetry and her Catholic practice. As for many 'memsahibs', the colonial existence has neither rewards nor comforts for her; and when she attracts the attention of Wilson, who claims to love her as her husband does not, her Catholic faith forbids a response.

Greene's personal love of Africa rarely seeps into the portrayal of this outpost of Empire in wartime. His life there in the Intelligence services was both frustrating and pointless, his most original idea (ultimately rejected) being that of a roaming brothel whose Madam would have contacts with Vichy France. The heat, the rats, the vultures all contribute to the hideousness of existence (its anti-poetry) which Louise must endure. Unlike her husband, for whom faith is at least a matter of an attempted dialogue with God, Louise is seen to practise Catholicism only as a formal discipline, an acceptance of obligations to confess and to attend Mass, with little consolation beyond the possibility of always starting again – at least so far as the reader can tell. While Scobie is conceived from within, his wife remains an observed character, whose anguish emerges only in what she says, and in the feelings Scobie ascribes to her. Greene's ear is finely attuned to the nuances of friendships between men, as here between Scobie and Yusuf, but he lacks the same inner ear for what is not sexual in the relations between men and women. Louise Scobie in her physical unattractiveness and loneliness comes to life more completely than the majority of Greene's women, but her portrait remains a projection of Scobie's male pity. For all the importance he attaches to sex, and relations between men and women, women remain largely outside Greene's creative range, except as the object of men's desires and failures.

During Louise Scobie's absence in South Africa, the survivors from a ship sunk at sea are brought ashore. Among them is a small girl, not more than 6 years old, who has survived forty days at sea but who will shortly die, with Scobie beside her. Her death becomes a re-enactment for him of the death of his own child when he could not be present. 'To be a human being one had to drink the cup. If one were lucky enough on one day, or cowardly on another, it was presented on a third occasion' (*HM* 125). Among the other survivors is Helen Rolt, 19 years old, who has lost her husband in the shipwreck. When Scobie goes to visit her in hospital she possesses little more than the stamp album her father had given her on her fourteenth birthday. The death of the child, and Helen's survival rekindle in Scobie a love which reflects the love God feels for his creation. In time Scobie becomes her lover, attempting secrecy in a place where nothing is secret, and exposing himself to the hostility of a society which sees the conflict between his faith and his behaviour as hypocrisy. To Helen, Catholicism is 'hooey', and his argument that he cannot marry her because as a Catholic he cannot have two wives only a source of bitterness. 'It doesn't stop you sleeping with me – it only stops you marrying me' (*HM* 179). None the less, when Scobie has killed himself, and Helen sleeps alone (after rejecting the advances of the oafish Bagster), 'she put her hand out beside her and touched the other pillow, as though perhaps after all there was one chance in a thousand that she was not alone, and if she were not alone now she would never be alone again' (*HM* 124). Love – the love of God for his creation and the reflection of this in human love – is suggested in this passage, which bears the imprint of his relationship with Catherine Walston. Greene was too considerable an artist to lift characters directly from life. Louise Scobie and Helen Rolt are not portraits of any of the women in his life, but they are projected out of his anguish at what could not be resolved. Catherine's solution was different from Scobie's but no less tragic: she died an alcoholic.

The sense of responsibility which Scobie cannot fulfil to Louise or Helen brings him close to despair. He grows weary of his religion, which offers no solution, except one which he cannot accept. The theological implications of Scobie's suicide are, as Evelyn Waugh pointed out in an early review, objectionable: 'He dies believing himself damned but also in an obscure way – at least in a way that is obscure to me – believing that he is offering his damnation as a loving sacrifice for others.'[8] God need no longer be concerned with his case, because to kill oneself is to commit the unpardonable sin of despair, and to ensure damnation. Waugh continues: 'To me the idea of willing my own damnation for the love of God is either a very loose poetical expression or a bad blasphemy, for the God who accepted that sacrifice would be neither just nor lovable.'[9] But Scobie does not exemplify doctrine; he lives in the abundant confusion of the human spirit, seeking justification for acts of which the motive, like God's own motive, remains inscrutable. The heart of the matter may be deserving of pity; not least because the facts are not known. 'If one knew, he wondered, the facts, would one have to feel pity even for the planets? if one reached what they called the heart of the matter?' (*HM* 124). In this sense his suicide represents not so much an unsatisfactory solution to a theological dilemma but a human solution to the feeling that life is unlivable.

Three months after *The Heart of the Matter* Greene was telling his wife that one good thing he had got out of America was 500 Nembutal tablets, and he could solve the problem with that. His wife did not accept the argument of friends that those who threatened suicide rarely did it. 'If he took an overdose, as he has often threatened, it would be like Scobie in *The Heart of the Matter* and – as in the book – I as his wife would be blamed by everyone.'[10] Greene, although he was often to feel he had no more to write, did not take his own life; but his novel records the disintegration of an inner life in which even faith can be used as the ally of the desire not to go on. Scobie's personality is not made less representative by his Catholicism. The falsity which Waugh rightly detects indicates a fracture in the attempt to find a meeting-point between what faith says about the world, and the experience of living in it. It was a novel the author did not care to reread.

By the time Greene came to write this novel, Christianity was fast losing its cultural force in the West. In choosing a quotation from Charles Péguy to act as an epigraph for *The Heart of the Matter*, Greene reminded his readers of a writer who had devoted much of his creative life to the mystery of charity; and arguably in times more receptive to it. Of all themes, none is perhaps more difficult.

4

Politics and Betrayal

The titles of two of Greene's earliest novels, *It's a Battlefield* (1934) and *England Made Me* (1935), indicate preoccupations which remain central in his later fiction. In *It's a Battlefield*, a campaign to win a reprieve for a bus driver convicted of murdering a policeman involves a conflict between the Communist activists and the power of the State. But the Communist leader, Mr Surrogate, would like to see the bus driver hang, so that he can be used as a 'martyr' to the Communist cause. The metaphor of the battlefield, with its connotations of confusion and disorder, is indicative of Greene's subversive vision, his dislike of political parties (he was a member of the Communist Party for three weeks in 1924), and his belief in the necessity for the writer of retaining the freedom to change sides. Writing, which is a form of action, is engaged with the heat of the battle.

The inner lives of individuals can never be assumed from their external allegiances; and, as with the ironically named Surrogate, those who might be thought to be sympathetic because opposed to repression turn out to be as bad as the oppressors. From Greene's first novel, the man within lay at the centre of Greene's interest, partly as a result of those childhood pressures which turned him into a writer, and partly because, as artist, he never separated the emotional and reflective man, from the practical active man. The integration of these aspects of personality, or more often the individual's lack of success in integrating them, offers Greene a way of projecting the individual and social turmoil of the mid-twentieth century.

With the very occasional exception, Greene regarded the politician as being amoral and corrupt because egoism, the desire for money and power, overcame the proper drive of politics, which should be 'the greater good of all'. In the pamphlet

J'accuse – the Darker Side of Nice (1982), Greene portrayed power as being in the hands not just of corrupt individuals, but of a criminal milieu, which included members of the judiciary and the police. Greene's exposure was prompted by the attempt to defend the daughter of his mistress from the violence of her husband and his associates. In his anger at the collusion between those who had power in Nice and its criminal élite, he returned his *Légion d'Honneur* to Paris. Greene did not win his case (the French court awarded libel damages against him); but in 1991 Jacques Médecin, who had continued in office as Mayor of Nice, was sentenced to prison for misusing public funds, and fled to Uruguay, where he became a seller of T-shirts.

Novelists who are obsessive may not always be right in their judgement of actual situations, though Zola, from whom Greene drew the title of his pamphlet, rightly championed Dreyfus. But Greene's polemic draws attention to a trend in political life of the late twentieth century, which threatens to bury the idea of public service, on which good government of any political complexion depends. Faction, a form of creative writing which has become increasingly popular, is dangerous in its manipulation of what is factually true, but none the less can be potent as an instrument of subversive awakening.

The title of Greene's other early novel, *England Made Me*, is suggestive in a quite different way. For all the places to which Greene travelled, and about which he wrote, his fiction is marked by a particular form of Englishness. Its characteristics are to be found in bias against ideology, a Protestant determination to form one's own view, and a liking for action. Greene never overcame his restlessness, his desire to be involved (he was an obsessive writer of letters to papers, especially *The Times*), and use his influence, where possible, in other countries' affairs. This became most marked in the last part of his life through his involvement in the politics of Central America. In *Getting to Know the General, the Story of an Involvement* (1984) he shows a characteristically English sympathy for the small country, Panama, resisting domination by the USA. His friendships, both in Panama and Nicaragua, however, show rather less political and human judgement. When asked by the *Washington Post* in 1988 about his association with the notorious General Noriega, he explained: 'An enemy of my enemy is my friend. And my enemy is Reagan.' As often with writers, Greene's imaginative prejudices determined his human and political judgements, blinding him to what he did not want to see.

The England which made him belonged to the age of Empire, and, for all his dislike of authoritarian regimes, his temperament was that of his time and his class. This shows as much in his attitude to women as it does in his attitude to political parties. But Greene's attitudes were marked by an oddity which left a distinctive mark on almost all he wrote, from *The Man Within* to his last novel, *The Captain and the Enemy*: an obsession with betrayal, made necessary by an incomplete commitment, by being a double agent, or by pressures which cannot be resolved because of divided loyalties. Emotion and idea are always involved in conflict.

No novel illustrates more clearly Greene's Englishness, with its recognition of the loneliness and incompleteness of ties, and the recognition of the unpredictable circumstances under which betrayal may come about, than *The Human Factor* (1978). The other novels considered in this chapter are set in Vietnam, Haiti and South America. *The Human Factor* is set in England, partly in Berkhamsted, which now becomes a refuge rather than a place of torment, as it had been in his childhood years, and partly in the London of men's clubs around St James's to which the members of the Intelligence Services belong. Greene's style in this novel has a spareness and austerity which reflect his assurance in his subject matter; and the majority of his characters are imagined with a hard clarity which comes only from deeply intuitive knowledge. For all the years Greene spent abroad, this was the terrain he knew best; and, like his friend Evelyn Waugh, he wrote about it with that inner ear for the nuance of behaviour, manners, and dialogue born of a national temperament in a particular period.

The secrecy of the Intelligence Services becomes in a more general sense a metaphor for society and social relationships. The compartments in which people live are made necessary by their occupations, but their occupation also signals a self-enclosure, which precludes any open social intercourse. Secrecy is a condition of social life, where deep feelings are never openly discussed or admitted. Only in the marriage between Castle and Sarah, the black woman whom he has helped to escape from apartheid South Africa, does any community of feeling exist, and there too it is vitiated by Castle's inability to tell her, until the dénouement, that he is a double agent.

Greene disliked giving interviews, and even to his biographer, Norman Sherry, gave away little that was not well known. This personal determination to defend his privacy, and to guard his private emotions from scrutiny, also characterizes his class and his nationality. English doors remain firmly closed unless prised open! In such a society, the human factor reveals itself sparingly; but this does not preclude either differentiation or judgement.

In Dr Percival, Greene creates a character upon whose face 'flames of Hell flicker' – a phrase used by Greene in his memorable essays on Henry James, whose religious sense of good and evil he admired and imitated.[1] Dr Percival has no compunction in devising a means of murdering Davis in a way which will escape detection. Davis is innocent of any betrayal, and he is sent to his death, without evidence, consideration, or remorse. In the secret society where Percival lives he is able to use his authority over life and death without fear of reprisal. When Castle has had to be spirited away to Moscow without his wife or his child, Percival takes Sarah out to lunch to warn her of the problems of joining Castle if she fails to cooperate.

> The waiter had come to clear their plates. Doctor Percival's was clean enough, but most of her portion had remained uneaten.
>
> 'What about an old English apple pie with cloves and a bit of cheese?' Doctor Percival asked, leaning seductively forward and speaking in a low voice as though he were naming the price he was prepared to pay for certain favours.
>
> 'No. Nothing. I don't want any more.'
>
> 'Oh dear, the bill then,' Doctor Percival told the waiter with disappointment, and when the waiter had gone he reproached her, 'Mrs Castle, you mustn't get angry. There's nothing personal in this. If you get angry you are sure to make the wrong decision. It's just an affair of boxes,' he began to elaborate, and then broke off as though for once he was finding that metaphor inapplicable. (*HF* 245–6)

This is a rare moment of self-irony for Percival, the murderer whose politics justify his crime, but who with English reticence would never think either word applicable to himself.

The metaphor is applicable to the novel as a whole, in which boxes of various kinds create the space between people which cannot be crossed. Greene, as he admitted, has little interest in houses as such; but he uses them to define the personal space which characterizes particular forms of loneliness and estrangement.

Colonel Daintry lives in a flat in St James's Street, as Greene himself did above Overton's Restaurant. In charge of internal security, he is compelled to find the mole in his section; but he lives without relish for the hunt or the kill. In his flat he eats sardines out of a tin, is separated from his wife, and has become a stranger to his daughter. When he visits his wife's flat for his daughter's wedding-party, he discovers it full of china owls, one of which he breaks, and is quickly thrown out. He has no life in common with his companions in the world outside the borders of security; and in his private life only the knowledge of failed relationships. But Daintry is also capable in a reserved English manner of a terrible moral anger: 'There was nothing clear enough in the cause to justify murder by mistake'.[1] He wants to resign from the firm, 'tired to death of secrecy and of errors which had to be covered up and not admitted' (HF 212).

Greene's epigraph from Conrad, whose influence shaped the first novel, The Man Within, sums up the central theme of this chapter: 'I only know that he who forms a tie is lost. The germ of corruption has entered his soul.' But the ties which arise out of nationality, class, education, and gender are formed in many respects before any consciousness of them exists; and they may come to be in conflict with ties formed later. Castle, the English Intelligence officer in apartheid South Africa, falls in love with a black woman and, in order to save her and her son from Boss, the secret police, engineers their escape with the help of the Communists, for whom he becomes in return a double agent. In betraying his country, he remains loyal to his love for a woman and her son. But he in turn will be betrayed by Moscow in its failure to lift Sarah and Sam out of the country. In politics, betrayal is of the essence, and its fruit the loneliness in which human beings live. The ending of The Human Factor, when Castle is allowed a brief phone call from Moscow to Sarah in England, remains among the bleakest Greene wrote, and suggestive of more important human truths than Pinkie's desire for revenge. 'She said, "Maurice, Maurice, please go on hoping," but in the long unbroken silence which followed she realised that the line to Moscow was dead' (HF 265).

Greene's subtlety in shaping the narrative perspective delays the identification of Castle as the mole until the novel is well advanced. The gradual unravelling of his secret also reveals the enforced isolation which living in a closed society involves, with its sadness and lack of human contact. And this too may be a comment on the life of the artist. In his essay on 'The Young Dickens', Green suggested that the creative writer perceives his world once and for all in childhood and adolescence, and his whole career is an attempt to illustrate his private world in terms of the great public world we all share. *The Human Factor* illustrates this better than any other of his novels; in it the loneliness and the betrayal of his early years infect, and at the same time define, a peculiarly English world, closed in on itself.

In French Indo-China at the end of colonial rule, Greene found a refuge from the insoluble intensity of his relationship with Catherine Walston. Out of his visits there he wrote *The Quiet American*: a novel which, in spite of its familiar touches – the English journalist whose Catholic wife will not divorce him – is vividly aware of global changes affecting or beginning to affect the second half of the twentieth century. While the French struggle against Communist insurgents in Vietnam, the Korean War further north is capturing the world's headlines. By comparison, Vietnam is still a local affair. But both represent that active front on which, in East and West, the ideological struggle to contain Communism is being fought. Through the character of the quiet American, Alden Pyle, Greene tells the story of the crucial shift between the period of European colonial rule and the new world dominated by US economic and foreign policy, which lacks direct knowledge of, or interest in, the countries it is seeking to influence. These are themes since taken up by Edward Said in *Orientalism* (1978) and *Culture and Imperialism* (1993).

Greene's dislike of ignorant American expansionism is tempered only by an ironic affection for the young man who becomes its agent and its victim. As always in Greene the novelist, the political issues cannot be separated from emotional conflict, since the ageing English journalist, Fowler, and the young American, Pyle, are both the lovers of the young Annamite girl, Phuong – a character whom Greene sees as an 'object' rather than a person in the new world order. What Phuong hopes for, and what Pyle offers, is marriage and a passport to the USA. What might seem a weakness in Greene's ability to create Phuong from within in fact portrays the shift from a romantic view of marriage to a practical and commercial contract of which the purpose is migration. Here the old order in both senses shows its contempt for the new.

> We used to speak of sterling qualities. Have we got to talk now about a dollar love? A dollar love, of course, would include marriage and Junior and Mother's Day, even though later it might include Reno or the Virgin Islands or wherever they go nowadays for their divorces. A dollar love had good intentions, a clear conscience and to hell with everybody.' (QA 63)

Alden Pyle's form of betrayal is the reverse of this; he is betrayed by his own naïvety, grounded in his unthinking acceptance of the books of York Harding (the book-based nature of US foreign policy is another of Said's themes in *Orientalism*), who, in his defence of democracy and the role of the West, has brainwashed Pyle into thinking he understands Vietnam. Pyle, unlike Fowler, believes in being involved; and this endows him with a courage blind to the dangers he is running, and oblivious to the way he is being used by those indifferent to human life. In the end, Fowler will be compelled to become *engagé*, and arrange for Pyle to be murdered before he causes more innocent women and children to die. Rather I should say at the beginning, for Greene with his skill in manipulating narrative and time begins with Pyle's disappearance. Pyle's betrayal of his friendship with Fowler in his love for Phuong is characterized by the same brave innocence as his politics. He braves the war zone, taking immense risks, to break the news of what has happened to Fowler. He cannot tell Phuong that he has fallen in love with her, without Fowler knowing. Pyle, as Fowler acknowledges, is sincere in his way, and also unknowing; until his death, others pay the price of his ignorance. The Third Force which he wants to create in Vietnam is simply used by others to further their ends, without reference to the cost in human life.

> Then someone asked him some stock question about the chances of the Government here ever beating the Vietminh and he said a Third Force could do it. There was always a Third Force to be found free from Communism and the taint of colonialism – national democracy he called it; you only had to find a leader and keep him safe from the old

colonial powers. (*QA* 124)

Fowler's increasing impatience with Pyle's half-baked ideas cannot be separated from his sexual jealousy that Phuong leaves him for Pyle. The politics of the book take their tone from its emotions. But with the deaths caused by a massive explosion in Saigon, in which Pyle is clearly implicated, Fowler's desire to remain politically detached ceases, even if his motives for arranging Pyle's death remain suspect. In this new political environment, the motives of the old colonialists, the factions within Vietnam, and the supporters of 'national democracy' are all seen as corrupt. The new world which is struggling to be born has no clarity; and Pyle's question to Fowler, 'are you playing straight?', little meaning. Greene's achievement lies in portraying the confusion of personal and national identities as symptomatic of the way the twentieth century was moving into another phase of cultural interrelationship (the global village was becoming all the time more apparent) and cultural uncertainty. Politics as seen in this novel are a matter of 'to hell with everyone else'. And Pyle's impossible standards, based on ignorance, are more dangerous to those attempting an ordinary life than to those who understand the rules of the game. As a political allegory, it exemplifies the old dictum, 'fools rush in where angels fear to tread'; but the novel also indicts the new economic interventionism (Pyle works for the Economic Aid Mission) trying to replace old-style colonialism. There is no doubt where Greene's sympathies as an Englishman lie.

In the foreword to *The Comedians*, Greene acknowledges that, as in *The End of the Affair* and *The Quiet American*, he has used a first-person narrative, while disclaiming any identify between himself and these narrators, 'I want to make it clear that the narrator of this tale, though his name is Brown, is not Greene.' More generally he defends the imaginary nature of his characters, 'A physical trait taken here, a habit of speech, an anecdote – they are boiled up in the kitchen of the unconscious and emerge unrecognizable even to the cook in most cases' (*Com.* 5).

In *The Comedians* the bond between personal emotions and political ideas which had created the lyric intensity in much of the earlier writing begins to be loosened. In the Haiti of Papa Doc, political oppression and the terrorism of the Tontons Macoute reflect a horror which is continuing and real; sexual relationships, however inadequate, seem in comparison part of a human comedy, especially at a time when 'fidelity is not to be expected'. As the narrator Brown learns, the trick of laughter is an advantage. This partial severance of the political and the emotional modifies Greene's style. As a narrative, *The Comedians* is less taughtly constructed, lacking the smouldering resentments of *The End of the Affair* and the remorse of *The Quiet American*. The affair between Brown and Martha, the wife of a South American ambassador, constantly thwarted or interrupted by the presence of her child, Angel, fails to generate any depth in Greene's writing because it lacks anguish. The attempt to contrast the horror and the comedy, while being of interest conceptually, does not fire Greene's imagination; and the resulting narrative lacks a sustained inner tension.

The changed political and cultural climate in which Greene was now writing suggests one way of accounting for this. In *The Power and the Glory* Greene could still conceive State suppression of the Catholic Church in terms of the struggle between the lieutenant and the whisky priest, between evolutionary socialist ideology, on the one hand, and metaphysical belief, on the other. In *The Comedians* ideological conflict has been reduced to the uncontrolled violence of the Tontons Macoute. In this there exists none of the belief in a better future which, however misguided and misapplied, sustains a residual sympathy for the lieutenant; here society has grown violent by the abuse of Presidential power, and the proximity of a USA willing to support almost any regime provided it keeps the Communists out. In a state where arbitrary violence and fear are the only instruments of government policy, betrayal ceases to have much meaning.

The theme is none the less sustained as an undercurrent in this new cultural context, where what is betrayed is not a faith but an underlying human dignity. In addition, Greene's attraction to danger as an antidote to the boredom of security has little of the internal vibrancy to be found in *A Gun for Sale* or *Brighton Rock*, because here he is confronting an actual political regime which he would like to see removed, as opposed to a haunting inner evil. As he admitted, *The Comedians* is the only one of his books which he began with the intention of expressing a point of view in order to fight – to fight the horror of Papa Doc's dictatorship. The virulence of Duvalier's response, in which he chastised Greene as a 'pervert', proved that the bullet found its mark.

In the character of Mr Smith, the presidential candidate from the USA (who polled 10,000 votes) Greene imagines, as he had with Alden Pyle, the possibility of a kind of innocence surviving in the modern political world. With Pyle, innocence and ignorance become corrupt and destructive partners. But Mr Smith's innocence, unlike Pyle's in that it cannot be used, signals a resistance to brutality, violence, and corruption which Papa Doc's regime lacks the power to break down. Smith's mission to bring vegetarianism to Haiti lies on the comic side of things; but his and his wife's courage when confronted by the Tontons Macoute reaffirms a human dignity and worth in danger of being trampled on.

> 'An ugly customer,' I said uneasily. Then I noticed that Mr Smith was returning the stare. One couldn't see how often the man blinked because of the dark glasses; he might easily have closed his eyes and rested them and we would not have known, yet it was Mr Smith's blue relentless gaze which won the day. (*Com*. 111)

At the close of the novel he will once again help the impecunious Brown, and defend the need not to feel ashamed of a fellow-countryman. 'In my state we still have a tradition of hospitality. When a man knocks on the door we don't ask him about his politics' (*Com*. 276). What is being defended here from betrayal lies beyond politics, but cannot amend what politics betrays.

This continuity of human dignity and decency is defended at another level by Dr Magiot in the letter which he writes to Brown shortly before his assassination: 'I implore you – a knock on the door may not allow me to finish this sentence, so take it as the last request of a dying man – if you have abandoned one faith, do not abandon all faith. There is always an alternative to the faith we lose. Or is it the same faith under another mask?' (*Com*. 286). The unanswered question, like much modern art, invites the reader to supply a response.

Apart from *The Human Factor*, *The Honorary Consul* was Greene's last major political novel. Greene expressed a special affection for it,

> because I've succeeded in showing how the characters change, evolve. *The Power and the Glory* was more like a seventeenth-century play in

which the actors symbolize a virtue or a vice, pride, pity, etc ... Now in *The Honorary Consul* the doctor evolves, the consul evolves, the priest too, up to a point. By the end of the novel, they have become different men.[2]

He also revealed how the setting of the novel began to grow in his imagination.

I had seen the town of Corrientes (the scene of *The Honorary Consul*) by chance from the river-boat taking me from Buenos Aires to Asuncion in Paraguay where I was working on *Travels with my Aunt*. Something in the atmosphere of this town struck my imagination – I don't know what it was. There was nothing to see, just a little harbour and a few houses, and yet a sort of surreptitious charm was already at work. There's an old saying locally that once you discover Corrientes you keep going back.[3]

What might have become the setting for a novel about life in a backwater proved, with Greene's instinctive sense of the contemporary, topical and dramatic. As he finished writing the book, the Tupamaros guerillas filled the headlines by kidnapping the British Ambassador in Montevideo.

The bungled kidnapping of the US ambassador in this town on the border between Paraguay and Argentina by opponents of General Stroessner's regime in Paraguay (they kidnap the politically insignificant Charley Fortnum, the Honorary British Consul, in his place) diminishes the political force of the novel, and allows Greene greater latitude in exploring the shifting viewpoints of his characters. Betrayal here does not mean some falling away from a basic human dignity, or an adherence to a misconceived political ideal, but occurs within gradations of human behaviour, neither wholly good nor bad. As often in Greene, the real evil (General Stroessner) is off-stage on a fishing holiday.

The novel's discursiveness, which moves to a tense and memorable climax, embraces reflections on literature and literary styles, making it among the most self-conscious of Greene's fictions. In treating South American *machismo* with irony, he also undercuts his own fictional world of brothels and sex, where women provide a good fuck and do not exist as individuals beyond that. The central character Dr Eduardo Plarr, who in the end will give his life for the Honorary Consul, while being his wife's lover and the father of her child, knows how to fuck but not how to love. Unlike Fowler in *The Quiet American*, who has his revenge on Pyle, Plarr attempts to atone for the love he cannot feel, and the jealousy which Fortnum's ability to do so arouses in him. As in *The Human Factor*, which followed it, Greene showed himself here able to write, however tentatively, about the possibility of human love.

A more moderate form of betrayal also touches the lives of these characters. Jorge Julio Saavedra, the author of *machismo* novels, feels himself to be betrayed by a young writer, Montez, whose work he has encouraged. In an article, Montez decries Saavedra's works as mediocre, and revenges himself on the man whose boring counsel he has been forced to listen to. Saavedra's style is heavy with the false poeticism which Greene disliked in his own early work; but he is a character depicted with a good deal of sympathy, and not just because of Greene's characteristic attraction towards failure. When Dr Plarr goes to visit Saavedra in his room, he

> 'felt much the same astonishment that he had felt in the *barrio* of the poor when he saw a young girl emerge in an immaculate white dress from a waterless hovel of mud and tin. He felt a new respect for Doctor Saavedra. His obsession with literature was not absurd whatever the quality of his books. He was willing to suffer poverty for its sake, and a disguised poverty was far worse to endure than an open one. The effort needed to polish his shoes, to press his suit.... Perhaps he would be remembered in the history of Argentine literature only in a footnote, but he would have deserved his footnote. The bareness of the room could be compared to the inextinguishable hunger of his literary obsession. (*HC* 162)

The artist, who is committed to something larger than himself, and remains true to that commitment whatever the personal cost, arouses Greene's admiration, just as he also remained sympathetic to Kim Philby after his defection to Moscow. What people do not betray has become as important in this narrative as what they do; and Greene's interest lies in the intention as much as the result.

Dr Plarr, summoned to take care of Charley Fortnum in the hut where the revolutionaries are hiding him, could betray them. 'While he lay sleepless in bed he had considered the possibility of disclosing all to the police, but that would be to condemn Leon and Aquino to almost certain death, probably Fortnum as well' (*HC* 85). As the perceptive Colonel of Police realizes, it is usually a friend one betrays in these circumstances. But Plarr does not betray them. Aquino, the hard-line revolutionary, claims to have betrayed three comrades to the CIA under interrogation; but his left-hand reveals three fingers missing. Rivas, the priest, who has left the Church and married, has broken all the rules but has remained faithful to a view of God with which he can live. God is to be pitied for what has happened to his creation. He tells Dr Plarr while they wait for the police ultimatum to expire: 'You believe in evolution, Eduardo, even though sometimes whole generations of men slip backwards to the beasts. It is a long struggle, and long suffering evolution, and I believe God is suffering the same evolution that we are, but perhaps with more pain' (*HC* 226). Within God, the day side and the night side are locked in struggle, but in the end the goodness within God will prevail. This Manichaean faith enables Rivas to do what he has to do, even if it means killing Fortnum. He does not betray his faith, but is betrayed by the police.

Against this background of waning and doubtful uncertainties, there stands the power of the General committed to not criticizing the Yankees. 'The General has one great quality, like Papa Doc used to have in Haiti. He is anti-communist' (*HC* 172). And so receives aid. In these ideological struggles between nations, the individual, often confused and uncertain, becomes the victim. The writer who perceives this has to be willing to 'cross over' because the victims are not always the same; and they become victims for reasons as different as Plarr's and Aquino's. There is a *mystique* as well as a *politique*, and to this in their different ways they have been true. In this, for Greene, lies the value of the human factor.

49

5

Abandonment and Survival

Graham Greene described *A Burnt-Out Case* as 'an attempt to give dramatic expression to various types of belief, half-belief, and non-belief, in the kind of setting, removed from world-politics, and household preoccupations, where such differences are felt acutely and find expression. This Congo is a region of the mind...' (*BOC*, Preface). Because all Greene's novels are born of the duel between feeling and thought, they also represent many different but similar Congos. Sometimes referred to as Greeneland, they are more interestingly seen as an area of human consciousness in which the absence of God leaves the psyche abandoned to its own internal debate, attempting to find a ground for its being. The pain to which such a struggle gives birth – a psychomachia, as it was once called – creates both a longing for release, a cessation of pain, and in the absence of suicide, the need to find a way of going on living. Greene believed the writer to be someone who always showed the inadequacy of the *status quo*; but the problem often presented itself to him – as it did to Ivan in Dostoevsky's *The Brothers Karamazov* – in the form of a temptation to return his entrance ticket.

About suicide, from a non-theological perspective, Dr Magiot in *The Comedians* makes a short discourse over the dead body of Dr Philipot, found in Brown's swimming pool. In Scobie's case, the matter was seen very differently, because suicide meant damnation.

> However great a man's fear of life...suicide remains the courageous act, the clear-headed act of a mathematician. The suicide has judged by the laws of chance – so many odds against one that to live will be more miserable than to die. His sense of mathematics is greater than his sense of survival. But think how a sense of survival must clamour to be heard at the last moment, what excuses it must present of a totally unscientific nature. (*Com*. 95)

50

A little later in the same novel, the counterfeit Major Jones offers Mr Brown a share in his next scheme for getting rich quick.

> 'What I offered you, old man, was net, not gross. All yours.''
> 'If I survived.'
> 'One always survives, old man' (*Com.* 209)

This sense of survival, against the odds, is often to be found in Greene's later fiction; and its stance is that of the late twentieth century. When Pyle and Fowler are trapped inside the watch-tower where death threatens every moment, Pyle attacks Fowler's lack of 'mental concepts':

> There's something you must believe in. Nobody can go on living without some belief.
> "Oh, I'm not a Berkeleian. I believe my back's against this wall. I believe there's a sten gun over there.' (*QA* 94)

Fowler, as often, uses his superior knowledge, and cultivation, against Pyle's idealism; but his rejection of Berkeleian idealism (the wall and the gun do exist) reflects his attitude towards journalism, and the immediate political world. Everyone's back is against a wall, and the sten gun, or death is always 'over there'.

In some of Greene's fiction, especially that of the later years, confrontation with death, and the absence of concepts, ideas, or feelings which can be used to shore up a sense of personal ruin, are countered in a characteristically English way with humour and a sense of life as a bawdy, if black adventure. Brown, the character closest to Greene in *The Comedians*, puts it like this:

> Now that I approached the end of life it was only my sense of humour that enabled me sometimes to believe in Him. Life was a comedy, not the tragedy for which I had been prepared, and it seemed to me that we were all on this boat with a Greek name...driven by an authoritative practical joke towards the extreme point of comedy. (*Com.* 32)

As Brown reflects, the purser of the Medea is blowing up French letters decorated with comic faces in coloured ink to serve in place of balloons for the party.

Often, though, the melancholy strain still predominates, as in Fowler's inability to deal with his own remorse: 'How I wished there existed someone to whom I could say I was sorry' (*QA* 189). Fowler will have to go on, survive as he can. Querry, the burnt-out case, will have his problem solved for him when he is killed.

A Burnt-Out Case, set in a leproserie in the Congo, is taken up with the problem of survival, physical and psychological; and, like Conrad's *The Heart of Darkness*, to which it owes a great deal, it concerns lives poised on the edge of extinction in both senses. Querry, the world-famous architect, has come a long way, and believes there is nowhere else for him to go. He has, as he says, no belief in a God; he is not even interested.

After two months in the leper colony, Querry has established – or thinks he has – a measure of natural confidence with his servant, Deo Gratias; but one night he disappears. Querry follows him into the forest, aware of the stupidity of his errand, and still convinced that it is always possible to go a little further. (While life and consciousness remain, the end of the road has never been reached, as the boat on the river reaches a point beyond which it cannot travel.) When Querry discovers Deo Gratias, he finds him half in, half out, of the swampy water, unable to move with his mutilated hands and feet. Querry realises he will die of fear, if left alone again, and spends the night beside him. What enables them both to survive is a lingering unspecified hope. In scenes like this, Greene's early love of adventure stories – of survival and improbable rescue – is used and transformed, so that even a name acquires a symbolic force. 'He called "Deo Gratias! Deo gratias!" above the noise of the insects, but the absurd name which sounded like an invocation in a church received no response' (*BOC* 55).

The leper's loss of sensation, and consequent inability to feel pain in affected parts of the body, brings with it the danger of injuries, which go unnoticed and uncared for. And so it is with Querry, who comes to the Catholic leproserie, with his capacity for feeling deadened. 'When desire is dead one cannot continue to make love. I've come to the end of desire and to the end of a vocation' (*BOC* 50). He claims to have felt no pain in twenty years. Belief of any sort, like the desire for women, has been worked out of his system. As an architect concerned with space, he is aware that his space is empty. Even if he could recover hope, it would come too late: 'An obsessional phrase bobbed up again, like a cork attached to some invisible fishing-net below the water, "Who cares? Who cares?"' (*BOC* 52).

Dr Colin, the unbeliever who wishes only Christianity would reduce the price of cortisone, warns him that a man cannot live with nothing but himself, or sooner or later he would kill himself.

'If he had enough interest,' Querry replies (*BOC* 52). Underlying Querry's sense of being a burnt-out case is his disgust with success. Greene himself admitted he was more drawn to failure than success – an attitude which reflects the perennial despair of many artists with their own work, but also, in a more general sense, what Auden meant when he wrote:

> Sing of human unsuccess
> In a rapture of distress.[1]

Against the failure of pity to restrain the savagery in human nature, which has disfigured the twentieth century, Querry's disgust seems a cry, not against achievement as such, but against the failure of achievement of whatever sort to redress the balance of human cruelty. None the less, Querry's desire to seclude himself in the leproserie, to resist the idea that it is possible to go any further (the boat which goes no further upstream is symbolic of his inner landscape), marks, as he knows, a desertion. Like the doctor who can treat no more patients in the tropical heat, he suffers the shame of someone who 'walks away from his tiny segment of the world's battlefield' (*BOC* 110). The beginning of his cure will come when once more he starts to feel pain.

Querry does not commit suicide; he is murdered by Rycker, the jealous husband, who wrongly suspects him of having made his wife pregnant. His rage and his hurt becomes uncontrolled when he also thinks Querry, *the* Querry, to be laughing at him – a mockery which in his insecurity he cannot tolerate. The dying Querry claims to have been laughing at himself, at the absurd, like the joker who has finally seen his role in the pack.

> 'He doesn't laugh easily,' the doctor said, and again there was a noise that resembled a distorted laugh.
> 'Absurd,' Querry said, 'this is absurd or else...', but what alternative, philosophical or psychological, he had in mind they never knew. (*BOC* 196)

François Mauriac, in his essay on Greene,[2] saw him as offering a defence against the absurdity preached by the contemporaries of Camus and Sartre. In *A Burnt-Out Case* Greene came closer than ever before to joining their camp. But in the brief final chapter, after Querry's death, Dr Colin claims, 'he'd learned to serve other people, you see, and laugh. An odd laugh, but it was a laugh all the same' (*BOC* 207). That odd laugh is to be heard in many of the later novels, as a means of entertaining (a word he used to categorize some of his fictions), and also as a means of survival.

'We have chosen nothing except to go on living', Brown reflects in *The Comedians*. In a manner characteristic of Greene's literariness, he goes on: 'rolled round on Earth's diurnal course, with rocks and stones and trees' (*Com.* 279). Wordsworth's pantheism matters less here than the sense of rootlessness, transience, and perpetual travelling recurrent in Greene's later fiction. 'The first colours touched the garden, deep green and then deep red – transience was my pigmentation; my roots would never go deep enough anywhere to make me a home or make me secure with love' (*Com.* 223).

The choice to go on living is sustained in both the fiction and the life, however, by a comic exuberance which overcomes the melancholy of a man at home everywhere and nowhere. The odd laugh becomes increasingly a compensation for the 'divine error' (God has been merely mistaken) of the world.

Greene told Fr Duran that he thought *Travels with my Aunt* his best book after *The Power and the Glory* because it was 'a serious and sad book which happens to be funny.'[3] The stage adaptation by Giles Havergal in 1991, in which all the parts were played by three male actors who constantly swapped roles, as in a theatrical mad hatter's tea-party, brought out this bizarre laughter – the product less of character than of attitude to life.

Henry Pulling, the retired bank manager, thinks he has settled down to a quiet existence, tending his dahlias until he meets his 'Aunt' Augusta at his Mother's funeral. Henry finds himself lured away from the security of his suburban home into a life of travel, where his aunt's enjoyment of sex, and her pleasure in outwitting the law, addict him in time to a life that is also *mouvemente*. A good deal in the novel reflects Greene's enjoyment of self-parody: as he admitted, 'my subject is my life'. And that subject contains his earlier novels, bringing him back here to the Orient Express and Brighton as settings. But this Brighton is no longer the home of gangs on the race-course; their place has been taken by a church for dogs in which the barking drowns out the prayers. Greene's attachment to the novel derived appropriately from his feeling that it represented a break with the past in having no obvious Catholic theme.

None the less this picaresque novel does have a very distinctive theme: survival. Aunt Augusta is sustained in her life by her love for Mr Visconti, with whom she is seen dancing serenely at the close. Visconti has always been a criminal, at one time disappearing with all her money, and later collaborating with the Nazis, but he knows how to survive.

> 'Mr Visconti, as I told you was not a man for fighting with knives or fists. A man who fights never survives long, and Mr Visconti was great at survival. Why, the old sod,' she said with tender delight, 'he survives to this moment. He must be eighty-four if he's a day.' (TA 118).

When, at the end, she invites Henry to share in their precarious existence in Paraguay, she tells him:

> 'Next week, when we have our Dakota, perhaps it will crash with you over Argentina... My dear Henry, if you live with us, you won't be edging day by day across to any last wall. The wall will find you of its own accord without your help, and every day you live will seem to you a kind of victory. "I was too sharp for it that time", you will say, when night comes, and afterwards you'll sleep well'. She said, 'I only hope the wall hasn't found Mr Visconti. If it has I will have to go out and look for it myself' (TA 225)

Travelling, not sitting still, is to be enjoyed; and the enjoyment of life sustains the desire to prolong it. This sense of enjoyment and taste for adventure are what Aunt Augusta gives to Henry, at first to his dismay destroying his love of dahlias, and then giving him a new identity. 'As I went upstairs to bed I felt myself to be a ghost returning home, transparent as water.... I was almost surprised to see that my image was visible in the glass' (TA 164).

Stylistically, *Travels with my Aunt* is a major achievement. Greene's assurance in creating a narrative voice for Henry Pulling works from the start to establish a settled identity which his travels with Aunt Augusta will gradually disrupt and transform. Greene's imagination is drawn to a comic anarchy, in which figures of authority are deflated by imaginative vitality. In spite of Visconti's collaboration with the Nazis, and the violence of the dictatorship in Paraguay, the novel is not preoccupied with right and wrong, good and evil; depth has been replaced by surface, the horror which is always real is largely hidden by the comic invention. But the resulting laughter is a way of surviving in a world where the horror exists. And the last laugh in this novel where Henry can still find books an antidote to foreign travel comes appropriately from Browning, the poet to whom Greene so often returned:

> God's in his Heaven –
> All's right with the world!

(TA 265)

In *Getting to Know the General*, Greene's own comic adventures with Chuchu – a sergeant in the Security forces of General Herrera, the President of Panama, who had solicited Greene's friendship – arouse a deeper unease because Chuchu belongs to the 'real' world, where the laughter of survival is never innocent. There, fictional conjuring cannot be used to conceal the writer at play in a dangerous liaison.

Greene models his short novel *Monsignor Quixote* on the epic romance of Cervantes: *The adventures of Don Quixote*, (and to a much lesser extent, because it is not picaresque, on Giovanni Guareschi's *The Little World of Don Camillo*). Like *The Honorary Consul*, in a comic mode, it comments on the art of fiction by making a 'real' character the descendant of his fictional forebear. Set in Spain, *Monsignor Quixote* draws upon Greene's travels with Fr Leopoldo Duran, who has written in his memoirs about the discussions of Catholicism and Marxism, the picnic lunches, and the mutual friendship which went into the making of this novel. Its stylistic unity is created out of a Quixotic humour, which sees the central character as neither the Catholic priest nor the Communist mayor, but Rocinante, the ancient Seat 600 in which they travel together. Their ability to continue on their journey together depends on Rocinante's ability to survive. Like the faith of the two men, Rocinante is often at her last gasp. From the first page, where the priest sets out to buy wine, until the climax, when Rocinante crashes into the monastery church at Osera, her performance shares with those who drive in her an idiosyncratic temperament, even a humanity to counterbalance their ideological disputes. What unites those who have not given up faith altogether is the comradeship of doubt; and Rocinante is the necessary vehicle in which this can occur, and be fostered.

> The Mayor put his hand for a moment on Father Quixote's shoulder, and Father Quixote could feel the electricity of affection in the touch. It's odd,

he thought, as he steered Rocinante with undue caution round a curve, how sharing a sense of doubt can bring men together even more than sharing a faith. The believer will fight another believer over a shade of difference: the doubter fights only with himself. (MQ 59)

The slowness of Rocinante makes a nonsense of distance; but like Don Quixote himself, who had never gone farther from La Mancha than the city of Barcelona, and had seemed to cover the whole immense area of Spain, Rocinante's journeying, like that of the two men, contains a metaphysical spaciousness which questions the age in which they live. Jet planes are for businessmen, while Rocinante remains 'of more value for a true traveller' (MQ 106). Surviving with any measure of humanity means not succumbing to the authoritative influence of Church or State or money itself. The bishop who disapproves of Quixote, and forbids him to celebrate Mass; the Guardia Civile who fire at Rocinante and cause her death; the rich Mexicans who return to Spain and corrupt the priests by offering money for the privilege of carrying the statue of the Virgin Mary in procession; all represent the powers which stand against the operation of grace, or the realization of the ideal of the Communist Manifesto. Survival means being saved from indifference, and going on with a journey which often seems absurd, without any clear notion of its end or its purpose. Before the great grey edifice of the monastery of the Osera monastery, 'a visitor has the impression of an abandoned island which has been colonised only recently by a small group of adventurers, who are now trying to make a home in the ruins of a past civilisation' (MQ 233). The monks who try to make a home are contrasted with the travellers who go on, however uncertainly, in Rocinante. But even for them, journey's end comes at last. When you come to the end of the longest road of all you have to lie down and take a rest – a rest from arguments and theories and fashions' (MQ 212). Even, too, from the comradeship and laughter of the journey.

Monsignor Quixote contains some of Greene's memorable comic writing, as when the priest and the mayor go to a pornographic film, misleadingly entitled *A Maiden's Prayer*, or when Quixote is imprisoned by the bishop, under suspicion, like his forebear, of being mad. Food and clothes – especially, the purple socks, the *pechera*, and the collar of the Monsignor – are used as instruments of a very English humour which lies between boyishness and

8. Sherry, *Life*, i. 566.
9. Duran, *Graham Greene*, 208.
10. Ibid. 209.
11. Allain, *The Other Man*, 143.
12. Hynes (ed.), *Graham Greene*, 170.

CHAPTER 3. 'A WRITER WHO HAPPENS TO BE A CATHOLIC'

1. Albert Camus, *Resistance, Rebellion and Death* (London: Hamish Hamilton, 1961), 50.
2. Arthur Miller, *Incident at Vichy* (New York, 1965), 66.
3. W. H. Auden, 'September 1, 1939', *Selected Poems* ed. Edward Mendelson (London: Faber, 1979), 88.
4. Norman Sherry, *The Life of Graham Greene*, i. *1904–1939*; ii., *1939–1955* (London: Cape, 1989–93), ii. 3.
5. Philip Stratford, *The Portable Graham Greene* (Harmondsworth: Penguin, 1977), 594.
6. Arthur Miller, Introduction, *Collected Plays* (London: Cresset, 1958), 7.
7. The words 'We're Catholics', which underline the point, appear only in the early editions.
8. Evelyn Waugh, in Samuel Hynes (ed.), *Graham Greene: A Collection of Critical Essays* (Engelwood Cliffs, NJ: Prentice Hall, 1973), 101.
9. Ibid.
10. Sherry, *Life*, ii. 287.

CHAPTER 4. POLITICS AND BETRAYAL

1. See Graham Greene, *Collected Essays* (London: Bodley Head, 1969), 21–54.
2. M.-F. Allain, *The Other Man: Conversations with Graham Greene*, trans. Guido Waldman (London: Bodley Head, 1983), 136.
3. Ibid. 64.

CHAPTER 5. ABANDONMENT AND SURVIVAL

1. W. H. Auden, 'In Memory of W. B. Yeats', *Selected Poems*, ed. Edward Mendelson (London: Faber, 1979), 83.
2. Samuel Hynes (ed.), *Graham Greene: A Collection of Critical Essays* (Engelwood Cliffs, NJ: Prentice Hall, 1973), 75–8.

3. Leopoldo Duran, *Graham Greene: Friend and Brother*, trans. Euan Cameron (London: HarperCollins, 1994), 240.
4. M.-F. Allain, *The Other Man: Conversations with Graham Greene*, trans. Guido Waldman (London: Bodley Head, 1983), 18.

Select Bibliography

WORKS BY GRAHAM GREENE

Babbling April (poems) (London: Blackwell, 1925).
The Man Within (London: Heinemann, 1929).
The Name of Action (London: Heinemann, 1930).
Rumour at Nightfall (London: Heinemann, 1931).
Stamboul Train (London: Heinemann, 1932).
It's a Battlefield (London: Heinemann, 1934).
England Made Me (London: Heinemann, 1935).
The Basement Room (London: Cresset Press, 1935).
Journey without Maps (London: Heinemann, 1936).
A Gun for Sale (London: Heinemann, 1936).
Brighton Rock (London: Heinemann, 1938).
The Lawless Roads (London: Heinemann, 1939).
The Confidential Agent (London: Heinemann, 1939).
The Power and the Glory (London: Heinemann, 1940).
The Ministry of Fear (London: Heinemann, 1943).
The Heart of the Matter (London: Heinemann, 1948).
The Third Man and *The Fallen Idol* (London: Heinemann, 1950).
The End of the Affair (London: Heinemann, 1951).
The Lost Childhood (London: Eyre and Spottiswoode, 1951).
The Living Room (London: Heinemann, 1953).
Twenty-One Stories (London: Heinemann, 1954).
The Quiet American (London: Heinemann, 1955).
Loser Takes All (London: Heinemann, 1955).
The Potting Shed (London: Heinemann, 1958).
Our Man in Havana (London: Heinemann, 1958).
The Complaisant Lover (London: Heinemann, 1959).
A Burnt-Out Case (London: Heinemann, 1961).
In Search of a Character: Two African Journals (London: Bodley Head, 1961).

A Sense of Reality (London: Bodley Head, 1963).

Carving a Statue (London: Bodley Head, 1964).

The Comedians (London: Bodley Head, 1966).

May we Borrow your Husband? and Other Comedies of Sexual Life, (London: Bodley Head, 1967).

Collected Essays (London: Bodley Head, 1969).

Travels with my Aunt (London: Bodley Head, 1969).

A Sort of Life (London: Bodley Head, 1971).

Collected Stories (London: Bodley Head, 1972).

The Pleasure Dome: Collected Film Criticism, 1935–40 (London: Secker & Warburg, 1972).

The Honorary Consul (London: Bodley Head, 1973).

Lord Rochester's Monkey (London: Bodley Head, 1974).

An Impossible Woman: The Memories of Dottoressa Moor (London: Bodley Head, 1975).

The Return of A. J. Raffles (London: Bodley Head, 1975).

The Human Factor (London: Bodley Head, 1978).

Dr Fischer of Geneva, or the Bomb Party (London: Bodley Head, 1980).

Ways of Escape (London: Bodley Head, 1980).

Monsignor Quixote (London: Bodley Head, 1982).

J'accuse – the Dark Side of Nice (Bodley Head, 1982).

Getting to Know the General (London: Bodley Head, 1985).

The Tenth Man (London: Bodley Head, 1985).

The Captain and the Enemy (London: Reinhardt Books, 1988).

The Last Word (London: Reinhardt Books, 1991).

A World of My Own: A Dream Diary (London: Reinhardt Books, 1992).

CRITICAL STUDIES

Adamson, Judith, *Graham Greene, The Dangerous Edge: Where Art and Politics Meet* (London: Macmillan, 1990).

Allain, M.-F., *The Other Man: Conversations with Graham Greene,* trans. Guido Waldman (London: Bodley Head, 1983).

Allott, Miriam, 'Surviving the Course, or a Novelist for all Seasons: Graham Greene's *The Honorary Consul*', in Jefferson, Douglas, and Martin, (eds.), *The Uses of Fiction: Essays on the Modern Novel in Honour of Arnold Kettle* (Milton Keynes: Open

University Press, 1982), 237–49.

Bawer, Bruce, 'Graham Greene: The Catholic Novels', *New Criterion*, 8/2 (Oct. 1989), 24–32.

—— 'Graham Greene: The Politics, *New Criterion*, 8/3 (Nov. 1989), 34–41.

Bloom, Harold (ed.), *Graham Greene: Modern Critical Views* (New York: Chelsea House, 1987).

Choi, Jae Suck, *Greene and Unamuno: Two Pilgrims to La Mancha* (New York: Peter Lang, 1990).

Couto, Maria, *Graham Greene, on the Frontier: Politics and Religion in the Novels* (Basingstoke: Macmillan, 1988).

Creasman, Boyd, 'Twigs in the Spokes: Graham Greene's Anti-Americanism', *Studies in the Humanities*, 14 (1987), 106–15.

Creese, Richard, 'Abstracting and Recording Narration in *The Good Soldier* and *The End of the Affair*', *Journal of Narrative Technique*, 16 (1986), 1–14.

—— 'Objects in Novels and the Fringe of Culture: Graham Greene and Alain Robbe-Grillet', *Comparative Literature*, 39 (1987), 58–73.

Davis, Elizabeth, *Graham Greene: The Artist as Critic* (Fredericton: York, 1984).

De Vinne, Christine, 'Truth and Falsehood in the Metaphors of *A Burnt-Out Case*', *English Studies*, 74 (1993), 445–50.

Desmond, John F., 'The Heart of (the) Matter: The Mystery of the Real in *Monsignor Quixote*', *Religion and Literature*, 22 (1990), 59–78.

Devereux, James A., 'Catholic Matters in the Correspondence of Evelyn Waugh and Graham Greene', *Journal of Modern Literature* 14 (1987), 111–26.

Diemert, Brian, 'Ida Arnold and the Detective Story: Reading *Brighton Rock*', *Twentieth Century Literature*, 38 (1992), 386–403.

—— 'The Pursuit of Justice: Graham Greene's Refiguring of the Detective Story in *It's a Battlefield*', *Papers on Language and Literature*, 30 (1994), 285–308.

Diephouse, Daniel, 'The Sense of Ends in Graham Greene and *The Power and the Glory*', *Journal of Narrative Technique*, 20 (1990), 22–41.

Donaghy, Henry J., 'Graham Greene's "Virtue of Disloyalty"', *Christianity and Literature*, 32 (1983), 31–7.

—— *Conversations with Graham Greene* (Jackson: University Press of Mississippi, 1992).

Duran, Leopoldo, *Graham Greene: Friend and Brother*, trans. Euan Cameron (London: HarperCollins, 1994).

Erdinast-Vulcan, Daphna, *Graham Greene's Childless Fathers* (Basingstoke: Macmillan, 1988).

Erlebach, Peter, and Stein, Thomas Michael, (eds.), *Graham Greene in Perspective: A Critical Symposium* (Frankfurt am Main and New York: P. Lang, 1991).

Falk, Quentin, *Travels in Greeneland: The Cinema of Graham Greene* (rev. edn. London: Quartet, 1990).

Ferns, C. S., 'Brown is not Greene: Narrative Role in *The Comedians*', *College Literature*, 12 (1985), 60–7.

Freis, Richard, 'Scobie's World', *Religion and Literature*, 24 (1992), 57–78.

Gaston, Georg M. A., *The Pursuit of Salvation: A Critical Guide to the Novels of Graham Greene* (Troy, NY: Whitston, 1984).

Hamada, Kazuie, 'Graham Greene, *The Power and the Glory:* A Comparative Essay with *Silence* by Shusaku Endo', in *Collected Essays*, 31, (Feb. 1988), 77–87.

Hansen, Niels Bugge, 'The I as Camera and Reflector: On Graham Greene's Use of First-Person Narrators' in Eric Jacobsen, Jorgen Erik Nielson, Bruce Chinies Ross, and James Stewart (eds.), *Studies in Modern Fiction: Presented to Bent Nordhjem on his 70th Birthday, 31 May 1990* (Copenhagen: Faculty of Humanities, University of Copenhagen, 1990), 49–67.

Henry, Patrick, 'Cervantes, Unamuno, and Graham Greene's *Monsignor Quixote*', *Comparative Literature Studies*, 23 (1986), 12–23.

—— 'Doubt and Certitude in *Monsignor Quixote*', *College Literature*, 12 (1985), 68–79.

Holderness, Graham, '"The Knight-Errant of Faith?" *Monsignor Quixote* as "Catholic Fiction"', *Literature and Theology*, 7 (1993), 259–83.

Hoskins, Robert, *Graham Greene: A Character Index and Guide* (New York: Garland, 1991).

Hynes, Samuel (ed.), *Graham Greene: A Collection of Critical Essays* (Engelwood Cliffs, NJ: Prentice Hall, 1973).

Kelly, Richard, *Graham Greene* (New York: Frederick Ungar, 1984).

—— *Graham Greene, A Study of the Short Fiction* (New York: Twayne, 1992).

Lodge, David, *Graham Greene* (New York: Columbia Essays on Modern Literature, 1966).

McCarthy, Patrick, 'Camus, Orwell and Greene: The Impossible Fascination of the Colonised', in Adele King (ed.), *Camus's L'Étranger: Fifty Years On* (New York: St Martin's, 1992), 221–31.

McEwan, Neil, 'Graham Greene (Basingstoke: Macmillan, 1988).

Maini, Irma, 'The Theme of Grace in *The Heart of the Matter*', *Literary Criterion*, 17 (1982), 51–9.

Man, Glenn, K. S., ' "The Third Man": Pulp Fiction and Art Film', *Literature-Film Quarterly*, 21 (1993), 171–7.

Miller, R. H., *Understanding Graham Greene* (Columbia: University of South Carolina, 1990).

Mockler, Anthony, *Graham Greene: Three Lives* (Arbroath: H. Mackay, 1994).

Monnier, Jean Yves, 'Myth and Reality: Graham Greene's View of Africa in *Journey without Maps*', *Commonwealth Essays and Studies*, 11 (1988), 61–9.

Monod, Sylvere, 'Le Chante de l'ennui: Graham Greene 1978–1982', *Études anglaises*, 36 (1983), 142–53.

Myers, Jeffrey (ed.), 'Graham Greene, a Revaluation: New Essays (London: Macmillan, 1990).

Nehring, Neil, 'Revolt into Style: Graham Greene Meets the Sex Pistols' *PMLA* 106 (1991), 222-37.

Newbury, Anthony, H., 'Graham Greene: Apostle of Commitment', *English Studies*, 30 (1992), 34–46.

O'Prey, Paul, *A Reader's Guide to Graham Greene* (London: Thames & Hudson, 1988).

Sharma, S. K., *Graham Greene; The Search for Belief* (New Delhi: Harman, 1990).

Sharrock, Roger, 'Graham Greene at the Heart of the Matter', *Essays and Studies*, 36 (1983), 56–78.

—— *Saints, Sinners, and Comedians: The Novels of Graham Greene* (Tunbridge Wells: Burns & Oates, 1984).

Shelden, Michael, *Graham Greene: The Man Within* (London: Heinemann, 1994).

Sherry, Norman, *The Life of Graham Greene*, i. *1904–1939*; ii. *1939–1955* (London: Cape, 1989–93).

Smith, Grahame, *The Achievement of Graham Greene* (Brighton: Harvester, 1986).

Spurling, John, *Graham Greene* (Contemporary Writers; London:

Methuen, 1983).

Stannard, Martin, 'In Search of Himselves: The Autobiographical Writings of Graham Greene', *Prose Studies*, 8 (1985), 139–55.

Stratford, Philip (ed.), *The Portable Graham Greene* (Harmondsworth: Penguin, 1977).

Swift, Bernard C., ' "The Dangerous Edge of Things": Mauriac, Greene and the Idea of the Catholic Novel', *Journal of European Studies*, 22, (1992), 111–26.

Symons, Julian, 'The Strength of Uncertainty: Graham Greene', *Literary Half-Yearly*, 24 (1983), 1–12.

Walker, Ronald, G., 'Graham Greene's Monkey: Contextualizing the Novelist's Biography of Lord Rochester', *Essays in Graham Greene*, 3 (1992), 43–53.

Walling, Gerald C., *Graham Greene: A Study of Four Dramas* (New York: P. Lang, 1991).

Wright, Andrew, 'Graham Greene's Parody of the Latin-American Novel', *Critica*, 2 (1990), 84–90.

Wyndham, Francis, *Graham Greene* (Writers and their Work; London, Longman, 1955).

Index

Africa, 13, 14, 24, 27, 33, 34
America, Central, 30, 38
    South, 30, 39
    United States of, 45
Antibes, 3
Argentina, 47
Aristides, 33
Auden, W. H., 25, 53

Barcelona, 57
Berkhamsted, 39
    School, 4
Bernanos, Georges, 21
Bloy, Léon, 25
Brighton, 54
Browning, Robert, 56
Buenos Aires, 47
Bunuel, Luis, 20

Calles, President, 27
Cameroons, the, 13
Camus, Albert, 53
    *Resistance, Rebellion and
    Death*, 24
Capra, Frank
    Mr Deeds Goes to Town, 19
Capri, 8
Carter, 4
Cervantes Saavedra, Miguel de
    *Don Quixote, The Adventures
    of*, 56
Claire, René, 19

Claudel, Paul, 21
Cloetta, Yvonne, 2, 8, 13
Communist Party, 37
Congo, the, 13, 52
Conrad, Joseph
    Heart of Darkness, 52
    Secret Agent, The, 14
Corrientes, 47
Cotten, Joseph, 17

Dayrell-Browning, Vivienne, 5, 6,
    7, 8, 27
Donne, John, 8
    Biathanatos, 32
Dostoevsky, Fyodor, 6, 9, 16
    Brothers Karamazov, The, 50
Dreyfus, Alfred, 38
Duran, Fr Leopoldo, 2, 3, 4, 15,
    56
Duvalier, Papa Doc, 44, 45, 46
Duvivier, Jean
    Carnet de Bal, Un, 20

Elgar, Edward, 6
Eliot, T. S., 19
Endo, Shusaku
    Silence, 28

First World War, 12
Fleming, Peter, 12
Franco, General Francisco, 58
French Riviera, 8

Freud, Sigmund, 13

Glover, Dorothy, 5, 7
Greene, Graham
    'Basement Room, The', 18
    Brighton Rock, 21–4, 26–8, 45
    Burnt-out Case, A, 13, 15, 50, 52–3
    Captain and the Enemy, The, 39
    Collected Essays, 16
    Comedians, The, 15, 44–6, 50–1, 54
    Doctor Fischer of Geneva or the Bomb Party, 16
    End of the Affair, The, 3, 5, 7, 14, 24–27, 44–5
    England Made Me, 37, 38
    Fallen Idol, The, 18
    Getting to Know the General, the Story of an Involvement, 38, 56,
    Gun for Sale, A, 45
    Heart of the Matter, The, 5, 7–9, 11, 13, 18, 21, 27, 32–6
    The Honorary Consul, The, 3, 15, 17, 46–9, 56
    Human Factor, The, 14, 16, 39–42, 46, 48
    'Is Christian Civilisation in Peril?', 28
    It's a Battlefield, 14–15, 37
    J'accuse – The Dark Side of Nice, 38
    Journey without Maps, 13
    Lawless Road, The, 9, 27
    Man Within, The, 14, 39, 41
    Monsignor Quixote, 3–4, 17, 20, 56–8
    Our Man in Havana, 5, 20
    Pleasure Dome, The, 19–20
    Power and the Glory, The, 5, 9, 14, 21, 27–32, 45–6, 54

The Quiet American, The, 14, 20, 42–5, 47, 51
Sense of Reality, A, 16
Sort of Life, A, 3
Stamboul Train, 14
Third Man, The, 17–18
Travels with my Aunt, 14, 20, 47, 54–5
'Under the Garden', 16, 17
Ways of Escape, 21, 22
World of My Own, A, 2, 11
'Young Dickens, The', 42
Guareschi, Giovanni
    Little World of Don Camillo, The, 56

Haggard, Rider
    King Solomon's Mines, 12
Haiti, 39, 44
Harston House, 16
Havergal, Giles, 54
Henty, G. A., 12
Hitler, Adolf, 24
Huxley, Aldous, 15

Indo-China, 42
Intelligence Services, 2, 3, 39
Ireland, 9

Jacobean dramatists, 22
James, Henry, 22, 40

Kenya, 13, 14
Koestler, Arthur
    Darkness at Noon, 31
Korean War, 42

Lang, Fritz, 20
Lawrence, D. H., 5
Légion d'Honneur, 38
Liberia, 13
Longfellow, Henry Wadsworth, 19
Lubitsch, Ernst, 19

machismo, 47, 48
Malaya, 14
Malraux, André, 11
Mau Mau, 13, 14
Mauriac, François, 21, 53
Médecin, Jacques, 38
Mexico, 3, 6, 22, 24, 27, 30
Miller, Arthur
    Collected Plays, 29
    Incident at Vichy, 25
Montevideo, 47
Moore, J. N., 6
Moscow, 48

Newman, Cardinal John Henry, 9
Nicaragua, 38
Night and Day, 19
Noriega, General, 38

Overton's Restaurant, 41
Oxford, 12

Panama, 38
Paraguay, 47, 55
Paris, 8
Pascal, Blaise, 11
Péguy, Charles, 36
Philby, Kim, 48
Pirandello, Luigi, 17

Reagan, Ronald, 38
Reed, Carol, 17, 18
Road Back, The, 19
Rochester, James Wilmot, Earl of,
    22

Said, Edward
    Culture and Imperialism, 42
    Orientalism, 42, 43
Sartre, Jean-Paul, 53

Scott, Sir Walter, 15
Second World War, 33
Shakespeare, William, 22
Sharrock, Roger
    Saints, Sinners and
    Comedians, 21
Shaw, George Bernard, 19
Sheldon, Michael, 2, 4, 6, 8, 21
Sherry, Norman, 2, 3, 4, 5, 40
South Africa, 39
Spain, 3, 21
Spark, Muriel, 21
Spectator, The, 19
Stroessner, General, 47

Times, The, 38
Tontons Macoute, 44, 45
Trollope, Anthony, 11
Tupamaros guerrillas, 47

Vienna, 18
Vietnam, 22, 39, 43

Walston, Catherine, 5, 7, 13, 25
Walston, Henry, 7, 9, 42
Wqshington Post, The, 38
Waugh, Evelyn, 6, 12, 21, 28, 35,
    39
Webster, John, 22
West Africa, 22
Weyman, Stanley, 12
Wheeler, 4
Wordsworth, William
    'Ode. Intimations of
    Immortality', 22
Wyler, William, 20

Yeats, W. B., 9

Zola, Émile, 38